C000157204

WINNING
STRATEGIES
WORKBOOK

Midgie Thompson

Acknowledgements

I would like to thank all the clients who have trusted me to be part of their journeys. It has been my pleasure to ride along with you and your feedback has been invaluable in helping me with my own life adventure.

I would like to thank Niki and Angela for your friendship, support and encouragement. Our shared journeys have been life changing.

Additional thanks goes to Catherine for your friendship, and for your inspiration and ideas in helping this workbook come to life.

And finally, thanks to Gabby for your support and wise words, and for encouraging me to keep going to get this workbook completed after having the idea for so long.

First Published in Great Britain 2016 by

Gabrielle Lea Publishing, London

© Copyright Midgie Thompson 2016

Cover and internal design by Catherine Hollingworth

Midgie Thompson asserts the moral right to be identified as the author of this work in accordance with sections 77 and 78 of the Copyright Designs and Patents Act 1988.

A CIP catalogue record for this book is available from the British Library.

All rights reserved. No part of this publication may be reproduced, stored in or introduced into a retrieval system, or transmitted, in any form, or by any means (electronic, mechanical, photocopying, recording or otherwise) without the prior written permission of the publisher.

This book is sold subject to the condition that it hall not, by way of trade or otherwise, be lent, resold, hired out, or otherwise circulated with the publishers prior consent in any form of binding or cover other than that in which it is published and without a similar condition including this condition being imposed on the subsequent purchasers.

ISBN: 978-0-9572186-6-6

Contents

To continuing the adventure!

*To all those who have encouraged me to dare,
to dream and to find the courage to take action.*

HOW YOU CAN USE THIS BOOK

This workbook brings out all the coaching questions that are contained within the 'Winning Strategies for Sports and Life' book and is somewhere you can keep all your answers in one spot. It's a great place to use for self-reflection and to remind yourself of the different aspects and elements that you identified as important or relevant to your life and to your goal. It is also for those busy clients who want to focus on the bottom line of questions that will help them achieve their goals.

You might choose to select one goal and work your way through all the steps. Alternatively, you might like to dip in and out of the different chapters when you want to sharpen up and work on a particular aspect of your mental skills.

With user-friendly exercises, including some new material, and plenty of space to make notes, the *Winning Strategies Workbook* will help you keep track of all your thoughts and ideas. If you want to write more or make additional notes for yourself, then it is suggested to get a notebook where you can keep these extra ideas in one place. Another option could be to use the space in the margins.

Whatever way you choose to approach things, you will further strengthen your mental skills, which can then have a positive ripple effect elsewhere in your life.

There are no hard and fast rules and no right and wrong answers. The questions are here to guide you along a journey of self-exploration. So, enjoy the journey and have fun!

INTRODUCTION

This workbook came about due to many of my clients asking me for an easy-to-use guide of the 'methodology' that I employ when I coach, and so after years of using these steps with sports and business clients to help them achieve peak levels of performance, I have finally put them down in writing in order to share them.

For those of you who are not familiar with how the 'Winning Strategies' process came about, I would like to share my own personal story of when I actually lived the steps described to help me recover from an illness and get me to the start line of my first marathon eleven months later.

In 1999, I became quite ill with a glandular fever type illness that caused me to be bedridden and unable to eat. Now, the fact that I was holding down two jobs and burning the proverbial candle at both ends, and in the middle, it was really not surprising. My body decided it did not want to play that game anymore! The lifestyle I was leading was neither healthy nor sustainable on so many levels.

As my health steadily improved and I started to regain my strength, I went from a time of struggling to simply walk down the street, because I was so weak, to being able to run a 10K race. The 10K came about due to a good friend, Lloyd, challenging me to run in a local race. He encouraged me, cajoled me and teased me into accepting the challenge with the goal to simply 'cross the finish line' regardless of how long it took. The gauntlet was thrown down and, of course, I had to pick it up; even though I didn't really believe I could do the distance, I always enjoyed a challenge.

Well, I did it! I ran my first 10K race just five months after I had been ill. I thought to myself, "If I can do this, what else can I do? What other goals can I set myself and achieve?"

After finishing that race, I was not happy with simply rejoining the human race, being a productive member of society and holding down a full-time job again (only one this time!), and so I decided to train and prepare for my first marathon. For this, I chose to return to my adopted hometown of Ottawa, Canada in May 2000.

Once that decision was made, I effectively lived all the principles I describe in the 'Winning Strategies for Sports and Life' book. I needed an excuse to help me live a healthier life and to take better care of myself, and the goal of running a marathon was certainly a strong incentive! I had no choice. I had to lead a healthy lifestyle in order to be able to perform at work as well as complete the required marathon training.

During my training, I had to overcome the doubts and fears I had about accomplishing such a challenging goal, but little by little I learned to believe in myself and that anything is possible if I put my mind to it. With the help, support and encouragement of my fellow running mates in Brighton, UK, I gradually built up my confidence.

Even though my confidence grew during training, when a race arrived in my marathon build up, I was a nervous wreck. I was afraid of so many things; I was afraid I would forget something, I was afraid I could not do 'it' and I was afraid that I wouldn't be good enough to do what I set out to do. All this nervousness was draining me of my energy, which in turn made me weak and tired even before I started to run. I knew I had to develop strategies to calm those pre-race nerves, focus on what was essential for me to run and have a pre-event routine that was reassuringly familiar.

When I actually got to that marathon eleven months after I had been bedridden and ill, I was ready with my personal mantra, which I repeated: "I CAN and I AM". I wanted to prove to myself, and to everyone who doubted me, that I could actually do it. And, I did it!

Afterwards, as I contemplated all that I had done to enable me to run my first marathon, I realized that the same approach could be used in many other areas in life where people wanted to switch themselves on and be the best they could be for a particular performance event, be it a race, a job interview, a presentation or many other situations. I started using these strategies with clients and saw great results.

This peak performance process is contained within the 'Winning Strategies for Sports and Life' book and this accompanying workbook incorporates all the coaching questions for each step with space to put your answers.

I hope it helps you in becoming the best you can be in your sports and in your life.

Midgie Thompson,
September 2016

Section 1
Getting Started

The aim of the Getting Started section is to provide the initial foundations to help you achieve peak levels in performance. Much like building a house, you need to start with strong foundations upon which to build the actual structure. In the context of performances, building strong foundations will help make all the rest so much easier and will help to ensure even greater success.

The first element in the foundations is getting clear on your goals and motivation. By taking time to clarify the outcome you want to bring about, you will then be able to align your efforts and your actions to help accomplish what you want to achieve. These goals will help provide a way to measure your own success against your own tape measure. Plus, it is all about focusing on your performance goals, rather than simply on the outcome goals. Exploring your reasons *why* you want to achieve a particular goal will help you put in whatever time is necessary to do what you need to do in order to achieve that goal. In addition, when the going gets tough and it might be hard to put in the work to achieve your goal, reminding yourself of the reasons can help.

The next foundation element towards peak performance is your values and beliefs. Achieving your goal and attaining peak levels in performances becomes easy and effortless when your actions are aligned with your values. Because you know clearly that what you are doing means something important to you, you will put more effort into it. Your values are the core of what is important to you; it is what you stand for as a person and what defines you as an individual. Your beliefs are how you view things and whether you believe something is possible or not. Your beliefs may be positive and empowering, or they may be negative and disempowering. By exploring your own beliefs that are related to your goal, you can identify any that might be holding you back. Once identified, you can then turn those limiting beliefs into positive, empowering ones.

Another element towards your foundations for peak performances is self-management. We all have different demands on our time, our energy and our attention, and fitting in the required training or preparation to achieve peak performances can be challenging. By looking at what those demands are, and exploring the effects of the people, places and things in your life, you will then be in a position to minimize anything that drains you and maximize anything that fuels you. This will enable you to be at your best for the day of your peak performance.

The final element in the foundations for peak levels of performance is life balance. This part is about taking a step back from your life to see the big picture of everything that you do and everything that is important to you. By getting clear about what is important to you and what your priorities are, and by evaluating the time you actually give to each of these areas, you can then make adjustments to align your activities with your priorities. Sometimes we say something is a priority, yet we do not devote the necessary time to it. When we get clear that something is indeed a priority, we can make the necessary time.

Once all the foundation elements are in place, you can then move onto the specific mental preparation skills and the event performance approaches to help you achieve peak levels of performance.

GOALS AND MOTIVATION

Excellence, in anything you do, comes from a commitment to yourself to go after your dreams. People who strive for excellence articulate a vision of where they want to go, what they want to achieve and clearly know the reasons why all this is important to them.

These successful individuals regularly set goals, align their activities towards those goals, monitor their progress on an ongoing basis and make adjustments to ensure they are on track to accomplish what they want to achieve.

The first step towards building strong foundations to help you achieve peak performances is to get clear as to the goals you want to achieve. According to Locke, Shaw, Saari and Latham (1981, cited in Garratt, 1999), the benefits of goals are:

- Creates focused attention
- Creates energy
- Creates long-term willingness to keep going
- Creates the opportunity for new learnings

In other words, the benefits of clearly defining your goals can help to increase your performance, motivation, focus, discipline and confidence. The more precisely and positively you define what you want, the easier it will be to take the necessary actions that will help, rather than hinder, your goals.

Sometimes it can be somewhat challenging, or even daunting, to decide what goal to actually pursue. So, let's start off with an easier step and start dreaming. When you have finished writing down all the things you have dreamt of being, doing and having, pick one that you want to pursue; one that you want to use this *Winning Strategies* process on in order to achieve peak performance levels.

Once you have chosen that goal, you will then articulate it using the SMART and PURE formulas. Afterwards, you will explore your motivation and your drivers to achieve that goal before making a plan. The plan is simply a guideline to follow and can highlight what needs to be done and by when or at what level of progress you need to be at by which point.

> *You are never too old to set another goal or to dream a new dream.*
> C. S. Lewis

Start dreaming

If you are already clear on the goal you want to achieve, that is great. However, I do encourage you to take some time and allow yourself to dream a little. We often do not take any time to think about, and dream about, all the possibilities we would like to be, do or have in our lives. So go on, make some time and allow your child-like imagination to run free and wild!

If you could be, do or have anything you wanted, and money was not an issue, nor failure a possibility, what would you be, do or have? Write down as many things that you can think of. Challenge yourself to write at least 100 things you dream about being, doing and having.

BE	DO	HAVE
	Ted Talk.	
	Murphys Law book	
	Write a fiction Story	
	Run a sub 20 5K	
	Win an award.	

> *The important thing is to dare to dream big, then take action.*
> Joe Girard

Now pick one to pursue as a goal

From all those dreams you have written down, which one do you want to pursue right now? Which one do you want to turn into a goal and take action on? Which one do you want to take through this *Winning Strategies* process and achieve peak levels of performance?

> *The question you should be asking is 'What would excite me?'*
> Timothy Ferriss

Taking those next steps ...
SMART, PURE and CLEAR goal setting

With that one goal you have chosen, it's time to write it out. Translating thoughts into written word, and then into actions, will help you along the way to being the best you can be. It also makes the goal seem more real, more tangible and more achievable.

Use the SMART acronym to write out more detail about your goal.

SPECIFIC / SIMPLE: What do you want to achieve? Where do you want to be at the end of the process or journey?

MILESTONES / MEASURABLE: What will be your smaller, milestone, steps? How will you know when you have achieved your goal? What evidence will you have?

ACHIEVABLE / ATTAINABLE: Do you have the resources to achieve your goal? Do you need to get additional support or resources to help you achieve your goal?

RESULTS / REALISTIC: Is the goal realistic and do you stand a good chance of achieving it? Is your goal in line with your other priorities and objectives?

TIMING: When will it happen? What is the timescale?

> *If you don't know exactly where you're going, how will you know when you get there?*
> Steve Maraboli

If you want to go even further in depth with writing out your goal, you may want to use the **PURE** and **CLEAR** goal-setting acronyms as well.

POSITIVE: Ensure that your goal is written down as a positive statement, as if you have already achieved it. If you have written something with a negative slant (such as something you do not want), ask yourself, what do I want instead?

UNDERSTOOD / UNDER YOUR CONTROL: Can you do all the steps yourself, or do you need someone else's input? Do you need to request their involvement or secure their availability for a particular time or have them complete a particular task?

RELEVANT / RIGHT SIZE: Is it relevant to where you are going and what you want to do? Is your goal the right size for you (is it manageable and doable)?

ETHICAL / ECOLOGICAL: What will be the effect on others when you achieve your outcome? Are there any unintended consequences, either negative or positive, of having this outcome?

The CLEAR acronym stands for:

CHALLENGING / COLLABORATIVE – Goals need to be challenging, which can provide an incentive to motivate. Within a business context, goals should encourage employees to work together collaboratively and in teams.

LIMITED / LEGAL – Goals should be limited in both scope and duration. All goals need to be legal, particularly in regulated industries.

EMOTIONAL – Goals should make an emotional connection, tapping into their energy and passion.

APPRECIABLE / APPROPRIATE – Large goals should be broken down into smaller goals so they can be accomplished more quickly and easily for long-term gain. Within business, goals need to be appropriate and relevant to an organization's context, direction, vision and purpose.

REFINABLE / RECORDED – Set goals with a headstrong and steadfast objective, but as new situations or information arise, give yourself permission to refine and modify your goals. Goals need to be written down and referenced in planning, action, progress and reviews. (*Economy*, 2016)

Although there is some overlap between the SMART, PURE and CLEAR elements, they can all help you further elaborate and expand upon your goal. If you want to keep things simple, just use the SMART formula as a start point.

How does your goal appear to you now? Does it seem clearer and more attainable? Does it feel as if it is more real now? What else might be needed to make it clearer and even more real?

If you can dream it, you can achieve it.
Zig Ziglar

Motivation

Motivation is your reason or reasons *why* you want to achieve a goal and will help you to make the investment of time and energy towards doing what you need to do in order to achieve it. So, take some time to really explore your motivation, as it will help you through difficult times when you might find it tough to get out there and take action.

> *Desire is the key to motivation, but it's determination and commitment that will enable you to attain success.*
> Mario Andretti

What are your reasons to pursue and achieve a particular goal?

What will it mean to you to achieve the goal?

What will happen when you get it?

How will achieving this goal affect other aspects of your life?

How is the outcome worth the time, effort and energy?

Based on the answers you have just written, what do they mean to you? What is their significance? How can you use them to keep you motivated?

> *When you want something,*
> *all the universe conspires in*
> *helping you to achieve it.*
> Paulo Coelho

Motivational drivers

Motivational drivers are those things that will either pull you towards or pull you away from something. Effectively, they act like magnets, pulling you towards your goal of something you want to achieve or pushing you away from a place where you might not want to be. This uncomfortable place provides the incentive to change.

Additionally, you might have internal or external motivating drivers. Internal drivers stem from your own sense of value you attribute to achieving a particular goal. This is what you think you want to achieve. An external driver might come from outside an individual such as from a coach, a boss or someone else. These drivers might be what you think others expect you to achieve.

The heart of human excellence often begins to beat when you discover a pursuit that absorbs you or gives you a sense of meaning, joy, or passion.

Terry Orlick

Looking at your list of reasons (written in previous section) why you want to achieve your goal, what are your drivers? Do your reasons stem from your own measures of success or has someone else defined them for you? Are they internal or external drivers?

So what are your motivating drivers? Are they acting like magnets drawing you towards something positive, or are they acting like a repellent pushing you away from a situation you do not want? Ideally, the drivers are internal and pull you towards your goal. What drivers can you come up with drawing you towards your goal?

Making a plan

Here is where you write out, as a rough plan, what you need to do and by when. This is like a timeline of actions or milestones to get you from where you are today to where you want to go. Rather than becoming overwhelmed by your goal and not knowing what to do, making a plan will help you see a way forward and then it is a question of taking one step at a time.

What needs to happen for you to achieve your goal? I suggest that you simply note down your ideas in a random order, perhaps using a mind map. There is no order or sequence for this step; it is simply ideas as they come to mind.

Once you have written down all your ideas about the possible steps, put them in an order of what needs to be done first, and then after that, and then after that. This becomes the timeline of steps you need to take in order to achieve your goal.

> *Focused, hard work is the real key to success. Keep your eyes on the goal, and just keep taking the next step towards completing it.*
>
> John Carmack

It is always a good idea to get input from others, just in case you have missed anything or to get ideas for improvements. Therefore, once you have written out your plan, consult with a trusted friend, coach or experienced person to get some input and ideas as to whether the plan could be further improved.

Finally …

Goal setting is your first step towards building your foundations and for achieving peak levels of performance. It provides a direction to focus your attention, energy and efforts. It helps you to become more successful, more quickly.

- Even if you have a clear goal in mind, just for fun, take some time to dream of the things you want to be, do and have in your life. With child-like playfulness let your imagination run wild. Even if you do not pick any of them to pursue, they might just go on your own bucket-list.

- Pick a goal that really excites you … that makes your eyes sparkle, your heart sing and your feet dance a little happy dance.

- Remember that motivation is like a magnet that can draw you forward until you achieve it.

- Focus on what you want, rather than on what you do not want.

- Pick a goal that you want to do for yourself, rather than for others.

- Remember that plans are a guideline of intended actions and achievements. However, remain flexible in case life distracts you and pulls you off course. If that happens, make adjustments along the way.

Notes and reflections

Here is some space to make any notes after having completed this section. How did you find the process? What insights did you gain? What thoughts do you have?

Life begins at the end of your comfort zone.

Neale Donald Walsch

VALUES AND BELIEFS

The next step in your *Winning Strategies* formula is to identify your values and beliefs related to your goal. Values are the core of what you do and what is important to you. They are what you stand for, what is important to you and how you live your life.

When your actions and activities are aligned with the core values that you consider as important, all your efforts and results become easier. However, if your values are not respected or if they are challenged, it might get you fired up with tension, frustration or even anger. For instance, if you value good health and vitality then it will be easier to eat well and exercise. Conversely, if for example you do not value personal challenge and being the best you can be, you may not push yourself as hard to train or to achieve the results you say you want to achieve.

Values might include such things as respect for self and others, honesty, love, and holding yourself accountable for your actions rather than blaming others. They could also include the value of happiness, peace, fun and adventure, stretching your comfort zones or staying safe within those comfort zones.

Your beliefs are your filters of how you see the world and what you believe is true or false. Some beliefs can be positive and empowering, while others can be negative and disempowering. The biggest factor in your ability to achieve peak performances is whether you believe you can do it or not. Even if you have never previously achieved what you are aiming to do, by remaining open to the possibility that you can achieve it, you set yourself up to making it become a likely reality.

We all have different beliefs because we all have different internal filters whereby we may delete, distort, or generalize what we see and how we see things. These filters may vary depending on the environment we grew up in, who our role models were, such as parents and teachers, and our experiences. The difference about these beliefs is whether they are helpful to us or not. Generally, beliefs are about ourselves, about our abilities, and about other people and things outside of us.

> *Values are a roadmap for action and they fuel the energy on which purpose is built.*
>
> James Loehr & Tony Schwartz

You can have positive and empowering beliefs that open you up to the possibilities of limitless potential, or alternatively, you can have beliefs that hinder you from being the best you can be and which limit your potential. It is as if you set yourself a ceiling of what is possible and think you can do no more. Often, these negative and limiting beliefs are buried deep within us and we may not even be conscious of them until we start digging around.

In relation to peak performances and your abilities, it is important to explore your beliefs, and to turn around or dispel any limiting ones to help you be the best you can be.

Values ... where do they come from?

I encourage you to explore your values about yourself, about work and specifically in relation to your goal. There are several different approaches here to help you identify them. Work through each set of questions and then review them all to see what they reveal about your core values.

What is important about what I do as an individual and within a work context? What else is important? Keep repeating the question, what else is important, until you cannot come up with any more answers. Really try to stretch yourself and find as many answers as you can of what is important.

In relation to my peak performance goal, what is important about achieving this goal? What else is important?

> *Only those who dare to fail greatly can ever achieve greatly.*
> Robert F. Kennedy

More help with identifying your values

For some, simply writing a list of values can be quite challenging because they have never really thought about what is important to them. If that is the case with you, then the following questions will help you even further. Even if you have easily identified your values, take some time to explore these questions and see what else might be revealed to you.

What would you say are your personal character strengths?

Who are you when you are at your best? What qualities are evident?

Imagine you are at your 100th birthday party with friends, family and colleagues. Everyone is standing up talking about what a difference you have made to their lives. What stories would they tell? What are the common elements or themes that emerge from the stories?

> *Whatever you can do, or dream you can, begin it. Boldness has genius, power and magic in it.*
>
> Johann Wolfgang von Goethe

When you sit quietly after this 100th birthday party and reflect upon your life and all the stories that were told, what would you say are the three most important lessons you learned about life and why are they so significant?

Think of several (at least three) individuals that you admire and respect. You may know these people personally or simply from their public presence. What are the top three qualities about each individual that you admire and respect the most?

What do the answers to those questions say about you? What core values can you draw from the answers?

Identify the times when you were the happiest, the most proud, the most fulfilled and the most satisfied. What were you doing and how were you being in these examples? What values were you living?

Even more help with values

Here is a list of some common core values. Take some time to review the list, highlight those words that resonate with you and then see which you might pick as your top 10 values. Some values you might decide to group together, which is fine, as long as they mean something to you.

Accountability	Discipline	Humility	Security
Accuracy	Discretion	Independence	Self-actualization
Achievement	Diversity	Ingenuity	Self-control
Adventurousness	Dynamism	Inner harmony	Selflessness
Altruism	Economy	Inquisitiveness	Self-reliance
Ambition	Effectiveness	Insightfulness	Sensitivity
Assertiveness	Efficiency	Intelligence	Serenity
Balance	Elegance	Intellectual status	Service
Being the best	Empathy	Intuition	Shrewdness
Belonging	Enjoyment	Joy	Simplicity
Boldness	Enthusiasm	Justice	Soundness
Calmness	Equality excellence	Leadership	Speed
Carefulness	Excitement	Legacy	Spontaneity
Challenge	Expertise	Love	Stability
Cheerfulness	Exploration	Loyalty	Strategic
Clear-mindedness	Expressiveness	Making a difference	Strength
Commitment	Fairness	Mastery	Structure
Community	Faith	Merit	Success
Compassion	Family-orientedness	Obedience	Support
Competitiveness	Fidelity	Openness	Teamwork
Consistency	Fitness	Order	Temperance
Contentment	Fluency	Originality	Thankfulness
Continuous	Focus	Patriotism	Thoroughness
Improvement	Freedom	Perfection	Thoughtfulness
Contribution	Fun	Piety	Timeliness
Control	Generosity	Positivity	Tolerance
Cooperation	Goodness	Practicality	Traditionalism
Correctness	Grace	Preparedness	Trustworthiness
Courtesy	Growth	Professionalism	Truth-seeking
Creativity	Happiness	Prudence	Understanding
Curiosity	Hard work	Quality-orientation	Uniqueness
Decisiveness	Health	Reliability	Unity
Dependability	Helping society	Resourcefulness	Usefulness
Determination	Holiness	Restraint	Vision
Devoutness	Honesty	Results-oriented	Vitality
Diligence	Honor	Rigor	

(extracted from *Mind Tools*, 2016)

Ranking values

After you have listed your values about yourself in general, in work and in relation to your goal, now take some time to rank them in order of importance. This ranking process is a testing one because it will challenge you to make some tough choices as to what is more important to you. Even when you say that they are all important, ranking values will help you later if you need to make some choices or decisions where there is a conflict.

Which is the most important value to me? If I could only have one value met, which one would that be?

If I had the previous value met, and could only have one more, which value would that be?

If I had the two previous values met, and could only have one more, which value would that be?

Continue ranking the values, asking the same questions as above, so you have your top 10 values in priority order.

1.	6.
2.	7.
3.	8.
4.	9.
5.	10.

Does that list look about right for the priority order of your values? If not, review your values and your list before rewriting in priority order. Having a clean and clear list of your top 10 priority values will help you for your future actions and decisions.

Aligning actions with your values

After you have looked at your values, it can then be an interesting exercise to see whether your actions are aligned with them. Sometimes our actions may be contradictory to what we say our values are and as a result conflict and stress arise.

When you review all your actions, are you living your life in accordance with what you say is important to you? If yes, that is great. If no, then what changes can you make?

When you reflect on how you are living your life and the actions you take in regards to your goal, are your actions and activities aligned with what is truly important to you?

Is there anything you could change or modify to ensure a better alignment between your actions and activities, and your values?

Are you doing anything that has little or no bearing on what is truly important to you?

*The only way to do great work
is to love what you do.*
Steve Jobs

Beliefs ...
empowering and disempowering

By exploring your beliefs related to your goal, you might uncover some that help, while others that hinder your ability to accomplish what you want to achieve. Beliefs are often those thoughts or things you say about yourself that start with 'I am ...'

On a personal level, these positive and empowering belief statements might include such things as *I am good enough*, *I am deserving*, *I am able*, and *I can do this* whereas negative or disempowering belief statements might be along the lines of *I can't do this*, *I can't achieve success*, *I don't deserve this*, and *I'm not good enough*, among so many others.

We also hold global beliefs, which are broad generalizations about how we view the world. These global beliefs often start with the following statements: *People are, Life is, The world is, People should / shouldn't, Women / Men are, Change is* or *The future is*. There are also *If/Then* beliefs. *If* something happens, *then* something else always happens.

> *You become*
> *what you believe.*
> Oprah Winfrey

So what are some of your beliefs about your goal? Write out all the thoughts you have about your ability to achieve the goal. Next, put the letter E for empowering and L for limiting beside each belief statement.

Finally, look at that list and review each of those belief statements. Make a few notes about what thoughts and feelings come up. Does it make you feel good or not so good about things? Where did that belief come from?

It's now time to examine any of those limiting beliefs (the ones you put L beside in the previous step) to determine whether there is any truth in them. Looking at each limiting belief statement, ask yourself the four simple questions from Byron Katie's *The Work* (www.thework.com):

1. Is it true?
2. Can you absolutely know that it is true?
3. How do you react, what happens, when you believe that thought? (Does that thought bring peace or stress into your life?)
4. Who would you be without that thought? (Who or what are you without that thought?)

Then, to turn that limiting belief around, ask yourself … how could the opposite be true? Write a statement, or several statements, that turns the negative belief into a positive one.

> *Once we believe in ourselves, we can risk curiosity, wonder, spontaneous delight, or any experience that reveals the human spirit.*
>
> e.e. cummings

Another exercise to help you shift any limiting beliefs is from Garratt (1999) whereby you complete statements related to your beliefs and thoughts regarding your goal.

We will use lack of confidence as the example and you can use any limiting belief you want to explore. Complete the following statements.

STEP 1 – I **lack confidence** …

When … (insert where and when you, for example, lack confidence.)

Because …

Before …

After …

While …

Whenever …

So that …

If …

Although …

In the same way that …

STEP 2 – I **want to have confidence** …

When …

Because …

Before …

After …

While …

Whenever …

So that …

If …

Although …

In the same way that …

STEP 3 – **I will be confident**

When …

Because …

Before …

After …

While …

Whenever …

So that …

If …

Although …

In the same way that …

By examining when, for instance, you are lacking confidence, followed on by what you would like to happen and what needs to happen, you will help loosen up those limiting beliefs.

As a final thought, ask yourself ... what else could I believe that would be more helpful to me in this situation?

You can have anything you want if you are willing to give up the belief that you can't have it.
Robert Anthony

Finally ...

By exploring your values and beliefs in this next step of your foundations, you are setting yourself up to ensure that your actions are aligned with what is truly important to you. It is also helping you to dispel any negative, limiting beliefs so that you can move forward positively and confidently in the knowledge that you can accomplish whatever you want to achieve.

- Values are the core of what is important to you and how you live your life. We are being truly authentic when we live by our values.

- Internal conflict arises when we live our lives a different way or do things that are not aligned with our values.

- Recalling examples of when you were the happiest, the most proud, the most fulfilled and the most satisfied gives you insights into you being at your best, and potentially your values.

- Are your actions aligned with your values? If not, what shifts might you make?

- Limiting beliefs are often hidden below the surface and we might not even be aware that they exist. Taking time to explore your beliefs will help shine a light on them.

- By shifting your limiting beliefs statements from when they happen to what you would like to happen and finally to what will happen, you are slowly shifting your thoughts to more positive and resourceful beliefs.

Notes and reflections

Here is some space to make any notes after having completed this section. How did you find the process? What insights did you gain? What thoughts do you have?

> *Always remember you are braver than you believe, stronger than you seem, and smarter than you think.*
> Christopher Robin

SELF-MANAGEMENT

In addition to the traditional time management strategies, which are so important when you have a big goal that you are pursuing, there are also energy management strategies that make a difference. This section will explore both time and energy management to help ensure that you make the time to prepare for your big event and also to make certain that you are fully fueled for the performance.

Many of us have busy lives these days and need to manage all of our roles and responsibilities to fit everything in. Nevertheless, a large number of us could make a few adjustments to improve our overall efficiency and effectiveness. By taking a moment to look at where you spend your time, you will be able to see more easily the areas where some shifts could be made and efficiencies gained. This exercise requires that you actually write down where you spend your time so that you can analyze the information.

Often when you take the time to complete what is traditionally referred to as a time audit, you are amazed at how you actually fit in all that you do in the time available. In these cases, it can sometimes be useful to look at ways in which things can be shifted around, tasks delegated and projects put on the back burner while you focus your time and attention on getting ready for that big event where you want to shine. The additional benefit of this written exercise is that you can use this information to compare with your overall priorities in life and see whether you are actually spending time on the things you said were important.

Another aspect of self-management is looking at your personal energy. Every activity you do in life takes 'energy'. Energy is expended when you get up in the morning, when you get ready for work, when you travel to work, and when you work, train and play. Can you recall a time when after being at home unwell, you started to feel better and decided to go back to work? How did that make you feel? Even though you may have been feeling well enough at home, going into work takes that bit more energy and can be exhausting. What about training when you are feeling unwell? How does that make you feel? These examples are just to raise your awareness of how much energy you have in different situations. Another way to help you understand the concept of energy is to recall an occasion when you spent time with someone who was negative and complaining. Did you come away feeling somewhat drained? Conversely, what about spending time with someone who was positive and buoyed? How did you feel after being with them?

By knowing what people, places and things drain you, and what fuels you, you can develop strategies to positively influence your performances. Whereas you might want to avoid or minimize contact with people, places or things that drain your energy before a big event, you might want to hang around people, places and things that fuel you.

> *The higher your energy level, the more efficient your body. The more efficient your body, the better you feel and the more you will use your talent to produce outstanding results.*
> Tony Robbins

Managing yourself and your time

The basic concept of time management is to identify what you have to do, know what your priorities are and keep focus to ensure that you take the necessary actions. Although this is a simple concept, it is not that easy to do. Many of us struggle with juggling many different roles and responsibilities both at work and at home, in addition to wanting to do other activities such as training for a big event or fulfilling a regular community commitment. So, let's take this one step at a time.

STEP 1: List all the activities you do and the time you spend on each

This list includes all the different roles and responsibilities you might have on a regular basis. I have included some suggestions; yet please feel free to add more.

- Work: What is your regular work pattern?

- Family time with partner and children: When do you spend time with them?

- Parents – visits and/or calls: How often and when do you make contact?

- Household chores: What is the frequency and duration?

- Training: When do you do your training/exercise? Is this an organized group or own your own?

- Meditation and Me-Time: How often and for how long?

- Friends: When do you see them and how often do you see them?

- Other clubs and activities, e.g. church, community groups, etc: When are these activities scheduled and what kind of commitment do you have to attend?

- List any other activities as appropriate for you.

STEP 2a: Actual priority list of activities from most important to least important

Looking at the list you made in STEP 1, write out the activities in your personal priority order from most important to least important. Remember, priority is based on what YOU deem as important, rather than what you think others say or think is important.

> *Freedom is not the absence of commitments, but the ability to choose – and commit myself to – what is best for me.*
>
> Paulo Coelho

STEP 2b: Real priority list of activities from the most amount of time to the least amount of time

Looking at the list you made in STEP 1, re-write this list based on time, from the most amount of time spent to the least amount of time.

STEP 2c: Compare the actual priority list to the real priority list

What insights or thoughts do you have when you compare the two? What changes might you make to realign your actual priorities with your real priorities?

STEP 3: Draft a weekly timetable

This provides a structure and outline of what you are going to do, and when, on a weekly basis. It does not have to be adhered to rigidly but provides guidance and helps you review how on track you are. Having some sort of regular schedule is a good step towards more effective self-management.

It is suggested that you start by putting down those activities where you have no flexibility such as school runs, work and perhaps group training sessions. Then, start adding in the other activities where you do have flexibility using your list of priorities as a basis for what gets put in the diary first.

> *He who every morning plans the transaction of the day and follows out that plan, carries a thread that will guide him through the maze of the most busy life.*
>
> Victor Hugo

	SUN	MON	TUE	WED	THUR	FRI	SAT
06H00							
09H00							
12H00							
15H00							
18H00							
21H00							

Personal energy management

Moving on from looking at your time management, the next step explores your personal energy. By recognizing the effect different people, places and things have on you and your energy, you can then put in place strategies to minimize what drains you and maximize what fuels you. Let's explore the concept of energy for a start to get you going.

Think about a time when you were with a friend who was being negative and pessimistic. How did you feel afterwards?

Now, think about a time when you were with a friend who was positive and optimistic? How did you feel afterwards?

Does one particular person leave you feeling tired and drained, and the other leave you feeling buoyant and uplifted? In what ways were you different or did you respond differently?

Recall a time when you were looking forward to some sort of activity. How did you feel? Recall a time when you were dreading something, feeling apprehensive or fearful. How did you feel then?

What differences did you notice between when you were looking forward to something and when you were not? What were your energy levels like?

The energy of the mind is the essence of life.

Aristotle

What fuels you and what drains you?

Go back to the list of activities you wrote in the time audit and give a subjective rating for each person, place and thing that you come into contact with. Do you feel drained or do you feel buoyed by the activities you do and the people you are with? You might consider a low / medium / high rating for each activity and how you feel doing the activity. Make some notes here for anything that stands out for you.

Did you notice any patterns? What were they? What can be done to change these patterns?

> *Passion is energy. Feel the power that comes from focusing on what excites you.*
> Oprah Winfrey

Doing something about it

Once you have identified those people, places and things that have an impact on you, now it's time to think about what you can do, all in view of making a positive difference for your performance.

For those activities that drain you, what can you do to minimize them?

- Which ones can you avoid altogether?

- Which ones can you get any assistance with to complete or delegate to someone else?

- How can you reduce the length of time you are exposed to the draining people, places or things?

- If you have to be exposed to the drainers, what different approach or attitude could you have to help minimize the draining effect?

- What things are you procrastinating about doing or making decisions about? What can you do now to get moving on them?

- Who can work with you to lessen the impact of any negative drains? Can you get someone to help you out?

Come up with ideas and strategies to minimize the things that drain you. Write these ideas down as a reminder for yourself.

For those activities that recharge you, what can you do to maximize them?

- How can you incorporate some sort of recharging activity into every day?

- What mechanisms need to be put in place so you can do what you need to do?

- What can you do that will help you feel more positive and recharged in just a few minutes?

- How often do you need regular recharging sessions such as a weekend away, a holiday or even a day off?

- How can you spend more time with those who make you feel good?

Come up with ideas and strategies to maximize the things that fuel you. Write these ideas down as a reminder for yourself.

Performance strategies

If you think specifically about your goal and your performance, is there anything else you could do to help you be at your best in terms of positive energy? What other specific strategies could be implemented to fuel your performance even more?

Finally …

Managing your time and managing your energy are essential for your everyday life, and for helping you to achieve peak levels of performance. By becoming more aware of your priority roles and responsibilities and reviewing where you spend your time, you can then have insight to make changes that work to your advantage and help you be the best you can be.

- Managing your time is more to do with managing yourself and where you place your attention, your efforts and your energy in the time that you have available.

- What we say our priorities are in life may, or may not, be reflected in how we actually spend our time.

- Looking at the total amount of time you spend on each activity and then list these activities from the most amount of time to the least amount of time might reveal different priorities than you actually thought.

- How different is your ideal weekly schedule compared to your actual week? See what adjustments could be made.

- When you start becoming aware of the people, places and things that recharge your energy or drain it, you almost unconsciously gravitate towards those people that help make you feel good.

Notes and reflections

Here is some space to make any notes after having completed this section. How did you find the process? What insights did you gain? What thoughts do you have?

> *To be fully engaged and perform optimally, you need to be physically energized, emotionally connected, mentally focused and spiritually aligned.*
>
> James Loehr and Tony Schwartz

LIFE BALANCE

It can be challenging to juggle all the competing demands on your time and energy. As you worked through the time and energy audits where you explored the people, places and things that either fuel you or drain you, you might have started thinking about what your priorities are and what is really important.

In this section, we take a closer look at those priorities before you decide whether any changes might need to be made. When you take a look at your priorities and then compare them to where you have been spending your time, you might more easily see whether your actions have been aligned and supportive of your big goal. Ensuring all your activities and efforts are aligned and helping support you in being the best you can be, precisely at that moment in time when you need it the most, is the key to peak performances.

The negative impact of living an unbalanced lifestyle can lead to an increase in stress and irritability, a decline in physical and mental health, low job satisfaction and morale, a reduction in productivity, and an increase in the rate of errors and accidents. Ultimately, it will have a negative impact on your ability to achieve peak levels of performances in whatever arena you wish to perform.

When you live a more balanced lifestyle, you help yourself to experience good physical and mental well-being, and have more energy, vitality, enthusiasm and motivation. In addition, you become more effective and efficient as well as achieve more success and satisfaction.

> *You have to decide what your highest priorities are and have the courage to say 'no' to other things. And the way you do that is by having a bigger 'yes' burning inside.*
>
> Stephen R. Covey

Identifying what's important

This WHEEL OF LIFE exercise is a fundamental step towards looking at your life and getting a 'big picture' perspective before even looking at where your goal fits into the scheme of things. Having done the time audit and the associated reflection, this may well now be an easier exercise to complete and you might have a clearer picture of the significant areas in your life. However, there may still be some things missing in your day-to-day life that are important to you.

STEP 1: Identify the most important areas in your life

What defines you as a person and what is important to you? Some ideas include: health/well-being, fitness/sports, children/partner/ friendships, finances/income/security, work/career, recreation/fun, religion/spirituality, community, travel/adventure and so on.

You might consider putting some individual areas such as family, friends or a special person into one global area under relationships. Other times, you might want to have separate groupings such as health, well-being and fitness depending on how important they are to you.

Below is a standard Wheel of Life image that you can use.

> *You will never feel truly satisfied by work until you are satisfied by life.*
> Heather Schuck

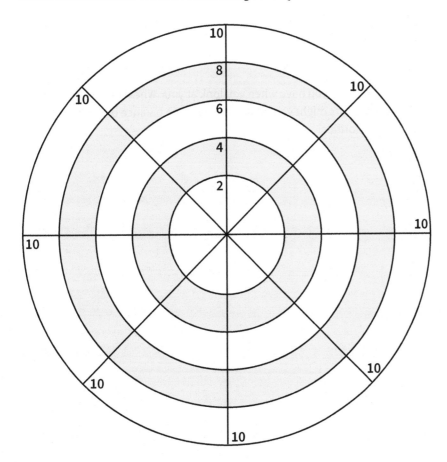

STEP 2: Rate your current level of satisfaction in each segment

Draw a line across each segment to represent your current level
of satisfaction in that area of your life, with 0 being at the center of
the circle and 10 at the outer rim. A rating of 0 means you are totally
unsatisfied and 10 means you are totally satisfied.

So, how does your Wheel of Life look to you? If the lines across
each segment were the outer rim of a wheel, how smooth would
your ride be?

What insights do you have when you look at your Wheel of Life? What
changes or shifts might you make to redress the balance or focus on
different priorities?

STEP 3: Describe what each area would be like
if you rated it a 10

Taking action in one area of your life and proactively doing
something to move you forward will generally give you a sense
of being in control and make you more positive about things. The
cascading benefit is that you will start to feel more positive about
other areas of your life as well and further actions become easier
to take.

Now, imagine that every segment on the wheel was a perfect 10.
What would you have? What would it look and feel like? What would
you be doing? Make notes for each of the segments as to what a
perfect 10 would look and feel like for you.

Could you make some changes in any these areas to move your current
satisfaction level to achieve a perfect 10? What action is required on
your part?

Actually making those changes

Thinking about possible changes is one thing, taking action is another. Yet, it is only by taking action and actually doing something about it that things will change. When you start making those changes, even small, baby-step changes, you will become happier and more satisfied with your life. This in turn will help fuel your performances.

So, what changes will you commit to taking action on? What changes can you make to help you move towards a better balance? Do you need to spend more time on certain areas and less on others? Who might you get involved to help you out? How might that work?

What needs to change to make this better? Describe all possible changes.

> *Life is about balance, and we all have to make the effort in areas that we can to enable us to make a difference.*
> Orlando Bloom

Who can make these changes? Identify the changes that you have control over, and those where someone else's input is required.

For those changes within your control, list the steps you need to take to achieve your changes, along with a timetable for taking action.

For those changes where someone else has influence, when can you make your request and what benefits will be in it for them to help you?

What needs to be put in place for these changes to work? What support or assistance from others is required?

What changes can you make to create a better balance? What actions will you actually take and what support mechanisms need to be in place for you to take those actions?

One day you will wake up and there won't be any more time to do the things you've always wanted. Do it now.

Paulo Coelho

Finally ...

Gaining the 'big picture' perspective on your life and your roles and responsibilities, and then making adjustments to live life in a more balanced, and happier, manner will help you to perform at a greater level. The graphical image of the Wheel of Life illustrates where you might make some changes in a positive direction. Following on from taking action, there will be a positive ripple effect.

- Getting a 'big picture' perspective on your life can help you see what is important to you and where your goal fits into things.

- The Wheel of Life exercise provides a graphical representation of your life and your levels of satisfaction. How smooth is your ride?

- The benefits of living life in a more balanced manner include improved physical and mental well-being, more energy and vitality, more enthusiasm and motivation, more effectiveness and efficiency, and more success and satisfaction.

- When you compare the Wheel of Life priorities with where you actually spend your time, the insights can be quite revealing and provide the incentive to make positive changes.

- To enable you to perform at your best and achieve peak levels in performance, you need to ensure that you make the necessary time for those priority activities.

- By focusing your time, your energy and your attention on what you need to do to achieve peak levels in performance, you do everything possible to ensure that it happens.

Notes and reflections

Here is some space to make any notes after having completed this section. How did you find the process? What insights did you gain? What thoughts do you have?

> *Grit is passion and perseverance. Grit is having stamina. Grit is sticking with your future, day-in, day-out. And working really hard to make that future a reality.*
>
> Angela Lee Duckworth

Section 2
Mental Preparation

This next section in the *Winning Strategies* process provides you with performance enhancing tools and techniques to take your performances from good to great, and then to outstanding. The following steps deal specifically with your mind, your thinking and your attitude. They will positively influence any performance.

We begin with the area of confidence. You can work on strengthening your confidence just as you would work on strengthening any muscle in your body. When your confidence levels are low, your performances will be lowered. Conversely, when your confidence levels are high, your performances will be higher. So, taking time to work on your confidence is worth the effort to raise your performances.

Another skill in this mental preparation area is dealing with your internal dialogue, that is, the inner voice, which talks to you all the time. Whether you pay attention to it or not, this ongoing commentary is still there playing in the background. At times that inner voice can be positive and supportive, whereas at other times it can be critical and unhelpful. By becoming more aware of what that inner voice is saying, you can effectively turn down or mute the volume on any negative analysis or unhelpful criticism and turn up the volume on positive commentary. It is much like having your own personal internal critic or cheerleader and only paying attention to the cheerleader.

Mental rehearsal, or visualization, is another tool to help you prepare and perform to the best of your abilities. In fact, this tool is the most powerful skill you can develop to assist you in performing at your best. Much research has been conducted on the power of visualizing something and how the brain actually reacts as if it were real. Therefore, from a performance perspective, if you mentally rehearse your performance repeatedly in a positive manner before the event, you are pre-programming yourself for success. When you get to the actual event, it is just a question of simply allowing your brain to do what you have trained it to do.

All of these mental preparation skills can be practiced and honed before the day when you really want them to count. This practice, much like the time spent rehearsing your particular skill and putting the hours in at the gym, will stand you in good stead when you get to your big event.

CONFIDENCE

Confidence is the belief in yourself to do what you want to do; it is the self-assurance that you are capable and prepared to take on the task or challenge you have set yourself up for; it is the certitude that you can do it – whatever 'it' may be. Confidence is based on your experiences and your perception of how you measure up. Yet, it is important to recognize that you need to define your own 'measures of success' rather than using other people's definition and view of what success means.

People with confidence have a 'can do' attitude and focus on the positives (even when there doesn't seem to be many). They will admit when they makes mistakes and will learn from them. A confident person will also be able to bounce back from setbacks, get back on track and continue on with taking action towards where they want to go.

Many factors and influences contribute towards your levels of confidence in what you do. These might include your family, friends, coaches, teachers, colleagues and bosses, among many others. Anyone who may have had an impact, either directly or indirectly, on your development will influence the degree of confidence you have.

You develop confidence in your skills based on feedback. Take for example when a child is learning to walk. They have many 'setbacks' with repeatedly falling, faltering and tentative steps holding onto something before being able to take their first steps on their own. The feedback children receive is full of encouragement, praise and admiration. They do not decide they won't try walking anymore; they keep on persisting until they get it. This is the same with any skill that we learn and develop. If we receive encouragement, praise and admiration, we will continue to practice until we get it right. We grow in confidence with each step we take before we are off and running.

Whether you are learning to walk, trying a new sport or about to give a big presentation, you may experience a certain lack of confidence. Yet, with practice you can develop a 'quiet confidence', a certain knowing that you can do it, and that whatever the outcome, you will be ok.

When it comes to peak performance, strengthening your confidence levels will not only help you to perform better, it will also help you to deal with any setbacks if they were to happen.

> *One important key to success is self-confidence. An important key to self-confidence is preparation.*
> Arthur Ashe

Confidence and performance

Before examining and exploring your confidence in relation to the big goal that you are using this *Winning Strategies* process on and to help you begin strengthening your confidence in the arena where you want it the most, we will first explore what your current confidence levels are like in all areas of your life.

Looking at different arenas in your life, where do you have good confidence levels? Where are you less confident?

For the areas where you have good confidence levels, how does that manifest? What are the signs or indicators that you are confident?

If you can think of areas where your confidence levels are not as strong as you would like, how does this manifest? What are the signs or indicators that your confidence levels are low?

> *Self-confidence can be learned, practiced, and mastered – just like any other skill. Once you master it, everything in your life will change for the better.*
>
> Barrie Davenport

Strengthening your confidence

Much like going to the gym to strengthen your body, you can also strengthen your 'confidence muscle' by doing some exercises. So let's start flexing some muscle!

If you were to imagine yourself with more confidence, how does it feel within you? What would you be doing differently?

What would being free from any negativity, fears or doubt be like? How would you act? What might you say to yourself?

Think of someone whom you admire and who seems to have lots of confidence. What sorts of things do they do? What sort of things do they say? How do they hold themselves?

How might you now act 'as if' you have strong and high levels of confidence, like the person you just thought about?

Reflect on recent successes or times when things went well. What things contributed to your success? What factors made a difference?

Reflect on a time when things did not go so well. What elements contributed to this experience?

What is the difference between these two situations – when things went well and when things did not go so well?

What are the key differences between the performances? Can you minimize or eliminate any factors that contributed to your poor performances, and ensure that you do all the things the same when you had good performances?

> *Confidence is a habit that can be developed by acting as if you already had the confidence you desire to have.*
> Brian Tracy

The way to develop self-confidence is to do the thing you fear and get a record of successful experiences behind you.

William
Jennings Bryan

Write a confidence resume

Much like having a CV listing out your education and experiences, a confidence resume chronicles your achievements and successes that make you feel good about you. This resume is a great way of giving yourself a confidence boost simply by reading through all the great things you have done and achieved.

List all of your achievements and successes in every area of your life. Note down even small things where you are pleased with what you did. These do not necessarily have to be major things.

When you look at this list, how does that make you feel? Does it give you a sense of pride that you have indeed done some rather amazing things? How are your confidence levels now?

What do you need to do to remind yourself of these achievements and successes?

Creating an anchor for confidence

An anchor is the connection between a trigger and a response. Anchoring happens naturally when feelings and emotions are strongly associated with a sight, a sound, words, gestures, and even tastes and smells. Then, when you see, hear, taste or smell the same thing again, the feelings and emotions return.

Let's begin with thinking of some anchors you probably already have. Can you recall hearing a particular song that makes you think of a special occasion? When you look back at holiday photos, how do you feel? Can you recall a particular smell such as your favorite food being cooked or baked? All these reactions and responses to the triggers are 'anchors' that you already have.

Now, let's create an anchor for your confidence.

First, identify a resourceful state that you want to create. A resourceful state is any thought, feeling or emotion that is positive and helps you. This could be more confidence, more concentration, increased relaxation or feelings of calmness, among many others. We are going to use confidence as our resourceful state for this exercise.

Then, you need to decide on what the anchor will be. What will be your own internal trigger? Just like when you enter a dark room and turn on the switch to get light, you need to have an internal light switch. The anchor may be a physical gesture, like pressing your thumb and first finger together, or it can be a visual image like a picture of you crossing that finish line looking strong. It might also be a simple word like 'power' or 'flow', depending on what works for you.

Next, imagine yourself feeling all those feelings, and while you are feeling those feelings of confidence, do the trigger gesture or recall that trigger image. This creates the connection between the trigger and the response, between the trigger and the feelings of confidence.

Repeat doing the anchor several times to really get the feeling in your body of what you want to feel. Then, repeat doing the anchor periodically to help remind yourself that it is there and to use it when needed.

What is your trigger to give you a boost of confidence? Write down as many details and sensations as possible to help you recall that feeling of confidence.

It is great to have a new tool in the toolbox, but you need to bring it out and use it for it to be effective. What will help you to remember to use this new confidence trigger? What other anchors might you want to create for yourself and what will be the triggers to use?

Dealing with setbacks

The reality of life is that we sometimes do not achieve what we want to achieve. We may experience setbacks or failure. This may have an impact on your confidence levels and your beliefs that you can do what you set out to do. When you are not experiencing the results you want, it is important to put things into perspective before making a plan of action for your next steps. Sometimes talking to a trusted friend, mentor or coach might help as well.

> *I am not a product of my circumstances. I am a product of my decisions.*
> Stephen Covey

Think of a time when you did not achieve what you wanted to achieve or had a setback. Describe what happened.

What outside influences may have had an impact on the results?

What was outside of your control that you can minimize for the next time? What was within your control that you can ensure you do again?

Regarding a goal, had you done all the preparation you needed to do? Had you been distracted by other more pressing things in your life, perhaps something much more important than what is going on in your performance arena? In the grand scheme of your life, where does this goal fit in?

When you experience a setback in the future, what can you do to remind yourself to gain a more positive perspective?

Finally …

Confidence is much like a muscle in the body, in that with practice it becomes stronger. We can all benefit from working on and strengthening our confidence muscle. Even when we experience setbacks and disappointments, we can still take away lessons that help put things into perspective and which we might take into consideration for the next time.

- You can draw upon times and situations where you had strong confidence to help you in times when you might not have as much confidence.

- Imagine you had unshakable confidence levels. What would you do differently? How would you act differently? What would you say to yourself differently?

- A 'confidence anchor' is something that you can easily recall and which will give you an immediate boost of 'feel-good feelings' and confidence.

- We all have fluctuations in our confidence levels and the difference is what we do with those feelings. Do we run and hide from them, or simply acknowledge them and carry on?

- Developing your resilience, or your 'bounce-back-abilities', will help you deal with any setbacks such as situations when you do not achieve what you want to achieve or when things do not go according to plan.

Notes and reflections

Here is some space to make any notes after having completed this section. How did you find the process? What insights did you gain? What thoughts do you have?

Confidence comes not from always being right but from not fearing to be wrong.
Peter T. McIntyre

INTERNAL DIALOGUE

We all have an ongoing internal chatter that talks to us. Even when we do not consciously pay attention to it, it is still going on and is still having an effect. When it comes to performance situations, this internal chatter may either assist or hinder your abilities to do the best you can do. The positive internal dialogue helps and supports you to perform well, whereas the negative internal dialogue can actually weaken your performance abilities.

Consider a critical parent, coach, boss or even friend versus an encouraging, positive person. Which one helps you to perform better? Which one motivates, inspires and makes you want to do your best? Even if the critical parent, coach or boss is not there, we may still say negative, critical and unhelpful things to ourselves. It is therefore imperative that we become more aware of this internal chatter to see whether it is being positive and supportive, or negative and critical. Then, we can do something about it, such as turning up the volume on the positive chatter and turning down or muting the volume on the negative things.

The reason to become aware of this chatter is because the words that are said have a very real and very literal effect on your physical body. If the words are positive, it will uplift you and help you to be at your best. If the words are negative, it will make your performance efforts even harder and limit your abilities.

Also, taking the time to examine this chatter and evaluating whether it is true or not is a good exercise to complete. When you can see the negative comments for what they are, and they are usually based on fear, you can turn them around or discard them. This does not stop those negative thoughts from popping up, but you will have the means to turn them around to positive ones that help rather than hinder your performances.

> *Successful people have fear, doubts, and worries. They just don't let these feelings stop them.*
> T. Harv Eker

Becoming aware of the chatter

Begin by noticing your own internal chatter. This heightens your awareness of what is going on, even when you may not be conscious that it is happening. From there, you can bring your focus to your performance arena and the goal you want to achieve, and become more aware of the internal dialogue that is going on.

Have you ever met someone you did not like? What sorts of things did you say to yourself about that person? Did you make up some sort of story or have a picture in your mind as to what they are like?

How many of you have gone to a game, a race, or even a training session, feeling negative before you even started? How was that game, that race or that training session? Did it seem harder than usual? What made it more challenging?

Now, think of a time when you were feeling pumped up and ready to go. How did things go then? What was the difference in the outcome that day?

Words and their effect

> *We become what we think about.*
> Earl Nightingale

Having explored your internal dialogue in a general context, now let's look at the effect of this internal dialogue by doing the 'chair exercise'. This exercise is simply to demonstrate the effect of words on your physical body. For athletes, who depend on their physical bodies to perform, this awareness is critical to help them achieve peak levels of performance. Yet, in any other performance situation, there is still an effect on the overall performance.

When doing this exercise, focus your attention on your body and how you feel as you are sitting down and as you are standing up.

1. Start the exercise in a seated position and just notice your physical body sensations. How are you sitting in the chair? Are you balanced or leaning in one direction? How do your shoulders feel? Is there any tension in your body?

2. Stand up from the seated position and just notice how it feels. Are you feeling balanced or do you favor one side? Do you stand up easily or do you have to almost haul yourself out of the seat? Return to the seated position.

3. Repeat to yourself 'I am tired, weak, listless, exhausted, afraid, I can't do this' or any other combination of 'negative' type words. Keep on repeating these words and stand up. Notice what happens with your body. How does it feel as you stand up? Return to the seated position.

4. Repeat to yourself 'I am strong, powerful, confident, energized, awesome, incredible, flowing' or any other combination of 'positive' type words. Keep on repeating these words and stand up. Notice what happens with your body. How does it feel as you stand up? Return to the seated position.

What did you notice when you stood up repeating the negative type of words? What did you notice when you were repeating the positive type of words?

What's going on

Experiencing what it is like on your physical body when you repeat 'negative' and 'positive' type words can be so revealing. Now, while performing, imagine what impact your words have in the middle of a game, a big event or an important performance such as a presentation or interview. Every time you have a negative type of thought, it has a detrimental effect on your body.

Start to notice your thoughts and repeatedly ask yourself 'what am I thinking about now?' What are your thoughts when it comes to your performances? What do you think happens when your thoughts jump around from one thing to the next?

Fear can be good, but it's not good when you have a goal and you're fearful of obstacles. We often get trapped by our fears, but anyone who has had success has failed before.

Queen Latifah

Write down all the thoughts you have about a particular performance situation. Afterwards, review them to identify the negative type of thoughts and ask yourself:

- Is it true? What information do I have for this thought?

- Do I have any doubt that the thought is true? How do I react when I believe that thought?

- What evidence exists that contradicts this thought?

- How often does this thought occur and have I been wrong about this thought before?

- What advice would I offer to a friend who had this thought?

- Who would I be without this thought?

Turning the negatives around

By taking the time to examine any negative thoughts you might have, and then having ideas as to how you can either turn things around or discard them, this will help you on the day of your big performance event. Remember, a performance event could be a sporting competition, a job interview, a presentation or any other situation where you want to be at your best.

What kind of things do you say to yourself before a big performance event? Are they positive and supportive or negative and critical? How can you turn them around so they are helpful and supportive? What sorts of positive things can you say to yourself instead?

> *If you hear a voice within you say 'you cannot paint,' then by all means paint and that voice will be silenced.*
>
> Vincent Van Gogh

NEGATIVE SELF-TALK	POSITIVE TURN-AROUND THOUGHT

Dealing with the chatter

Many of us have this negative chatter going on, but when we can shine a light on it and examine it, it loses its strength to negatively affect us and our performance abilities. Therefore, by reflecting on your past performances and the types of things you have said to yourself, you can spot patterns and situation. This then provides an opportunity to explore that situation in more depth and to do something about it, that is, to turn the negative chatter into positive self-talk.

When you think back to your past performances, recall your thoughts when you were performing at your best. What were your thoughts when you were performing at your less than optimal level?

Are there any patterns between performances? What might be the connections?

What trends are you noticing and where? Ask for proof. Is there any evidence to confirm it is a true statement?

What can you do to remind yourself to switch your thoughts to more supportive ones when you notice they are less than positive?

> *Obstacles don't have to stop you. If you run into a wall, don't turn around and give up. Figure out how to climb it, go through it or work around it.*
> Michael Jordan

Finally ...

Our internal dialogue has a big impact on our ability to perform. However, we are often not even aware of what it is saying. Taking time to examine what sorts of things we say to ourselves when things go well, or not so well, is a step in the direction to making changes. By ensuring that your internal dialogue is as positive and supportive as possible, it will make a big difference to how you feel about yourself and your performances.

- Words have a very real and a very physical effect on your body, so for an athlete, this is critical. Make sure that what you say to yourself is affirmative and encouraging.

- When you start noticing what your internal dialogue is saying, you can begin challenging the thoughts by asking whether they are true and whether there is any real evidence to back them up.

- If a friend says the same negative type of statement, help them turn it into a more positive one.

- Take a step back and examine all the things you say to yourself in an objective manner in order to identify which ones you can disregard as having no basis in truth.

- Become your own cheerleader to help encourage you to be your best. (Pompons are optional!)

Notes and reflections

Here is some space to make any notes after having completed this section. How did you find the process? What insights did you gain? What thoughts do you have?

> *Your opponent, in the end, is never really the (other) player. Your opponent is yourself, your negative internal voices, your level of determination.*
>
> Grace Lichtenstein

MENTAL REHEARSAL

Most athletes want to be as prepared as possible for their events in order to perform at their best. They want their training to have gone according to plan and they want their bodies to be fit, strong and healthy (injury free). All the preparation they have done will most certainly help to calm any nerves, doubts and fears as it can reassure them that they are ready to take on the challenge and do what they have set out to do. However, when they do not feel prepared for their event, the levels of stress, anxiety and tension can rise, and as a result, this can negatively impact on their performance abilities.

Part of the preparation that an athlete can carry out is mental rehearsal. Much like actors rehearse a play before they perform it in front of a live audience, athletes can rehearse their performances as well. Mental rehearsal is also referred to as visualization whereby you see yourself doing what you are about to do.

Grout and Perrin (2004, p. 153) say "to make the visualization as powerful as possible, you should be seeing the experience through your own eyes – rather than watching yourself as if on a screen. You should also engage all your senses". The more powerfully you can imagine a situation, the more likely you will feel as if it were real. So, when you get to the actual event, your brain will think it has already 'been there, done that'.

Mental rehearsal also provides you with the opportunity to go through possibilities of what might happen and deal with unexpected situations. Ideally, you want to rehearse best-case scenarios, yet equally important is to rehearse how you might handle other scenarios that are not 'best-case'. By practicing different scenarios in your mind, you are actually pre-programming yourself to effectively handle and manage whatever comes up on the day. If something does happen that is not in your best-case scenario plan, you will have more ideas that you can call upon to help devise a solution on the spot.

> *Ordinary people believe only in the possible. Extraordinary people visualize not what is possible or probable, but rather what is impossible. And by visualizing the impossible, they begin to see it as possible.*
>
> Cherie Carter-Scot

What to rehearse

Deciding on what to rehearse will be unique and individual to you. Some people rehearse their performance starting a week before the actual event, and others, a day before. They know what they will and will not do, and the steps they need to take. Then, on the day of the performance, they will rehearse everything and anything, from start to finish.

What actions do you need to take? Write down everything you need to do, from when you wake up, to travelling to the event, to when the event starts, during the event and all the way to the finish. You might decide to use the 'backward planning method' and start from the end and work backwards as to all the previous steps you needed to take to get you to the end.

- What will you see? Describe in rich detail all that you will see.

- What will you hear? From others? From yourself? Describe the things that you will say to others and to yourself. Remember to keep it positive.

- What might you smell or taste? Imagine the sensations as you smell and taste what it is like being there at your performance.

- How might you feel within your body? How will you be holding yourself, standing and walking? Describe the sensations after you have achieved your goal.

- Write out the sequence of events from start to finish. Then, as if you are watching a movie of you performing at your event, see yourself executing it and use all your senses to imagine really being there and doing it.

- Once you have watched this movie, now imagine stepping onto the screen and into your shoes. Run the movie again from start to finish and experience all that you will experience.

- Remember to watch and experience the movie several times prior to the actual day of your performance to help program yourself for success.

- What are the key markers or milestones to remember? What is happening at these points?

What the mind can conceive and believe it can achieve.

Napoleon Hill

Finally ...

Mental rehearsal, also referred to as visualization, is a very powerful tool in any performer's toolbox. Because the human brain does not distinguish the difference between what is real and what is imagined, you can effectively 'trick' the brain into believing that it has 'been there and done that' for your best ever performance.

- Much like actors rehearse a play before opening night, you can rehearse your 'play' for your performance.

- By imagining different scenarios in your mind (all those 'what ifs'), you are actually pre-programming yourself to effectively handle and manage whatever comes up on the day of your performance.

- Mental rehearsal helps to calm performance nerves because you will have mentally experienced the performance before you have had the actual physical experience.

- When you mentally rehearse your performance, make sure you see what you will see, hear what you will hear (both externally and internally) and feel what you will feel. For an even stronger experience, add in tastes and smells.

- Mental preparation is like doing a warm up before you exercise as it helps prepare the body to perform at its best.

Notes and reflections

Here is some space to make any notes after having completed this section. How did you find the process? What insights did you gain? What thoughts do you have?

> *To accomplish great things we must first dream, then visualize, then plan ... believe ... act.*
>
> Alfred A. Montapert

Additional notes

Section 3
Event Performance

This next section in the *Winning Strategies* peak performance process aims to introduce you to the skills, strategies and techniques that you can use on the day of your event to help you be the best you can be. These additional strategies need to be practiced before your event so that you can use them effortlessly on the actual day.

One of the key skills is relaxation. The ability to relax is critical for an athlete to perform more effectively and anyone else who wants to be able to think more clearly and perform more effectively. Being able to instantly and effortlessly relax with one simple breath, is a skill that with practice will become easy and will help you in many different situations where nerves start to arise. Some nervous tension is good as it can excite you and fire you up to perform. However, when the balance tips towards the 'negative' side of stress it can actually hinder your performance.

Another element towards helping you achieve peak performances is routine. Many of us get up each day and go about life almost on autopilot. This is particularly true with regards to getting up and out of the house to go to work. We do not have to think too much about what we are doing; we simply do what is necessary to arrive at work on time. Once at work, we then switch our brains on to function in that environment. In a performance situation, having a routine that is familiar to you, so you are effectively on autopilot, can similarly assist you and help reduce your sense of stress. It can also help athletes to 'get into the zone' for peak levels of performance.

The last skill in this section on event performance is regarding focus. It is important to pay attention only to those things that positively contribute towards your performance and to disregard those things that can detract from it. By maintaining your focus on task-relevant details, you are effectively keeping your attention and energy on things that help you perform, whereas when you start paying attention to non-task-relevant things it can actually detract from your abilities.

RELAXATION

In order to be able to perform to the best of your abilities, you need to become aware of the fine balance between good, positive stress that fuels you up and sharpens your focus and negative, detrimental stress that can inhibit you. When you are on the positive side of stress, you are more easily in that flow state and your body can do what you have trained it to do.

Unfortunately, many performers get so anxious before their big event that their nerves literally detract from their ability to be the best they can be. By learning how to use the energy from those nerves and channeling it towards a positive result, that energy will help fuel your performances rather than detract from them.

Understanding the effects of stress on the body, and therefore on performance abilities, can be the first step towards taking action to reduce any tension or anxiety. Start by recognizing the signs when your body is in a negatively stressed state and then learn techniques and procedures to deal with it. Releasing negative stress is beneficial to all individuals regardless of their performance arena. Additionally, take time to identify the people, places and things that add to those stress feelings and put in place strategies to either minimize them, let them go or turn them around.

Specific exercises like progressive muscle relaxation, 'one conscious breath', anchoring or 'grounding and calming' can all help to take the edge off negative stress. This can then free up the body to be more fluid and perform how you have trained it to perform.

Being relaxed, at peace with yourself, confident, emotionally neutral, loose, and free-floating – these are the keys to successful performance in almost everything.

Wayne W. Dyer

What are your stressors?

Before putting in place coping methods, it is important to take the time to identify the people, places or things that usually have a negative impact on your stress levels before your event. From there, you can then look at what elements you can and cannot control before establishing strategies to either eliminate, avoid or minimize them.

> *Some people thrive under pressure, but pressure can also ruin your performance, it can push you down angles which you don't want to go.*
>
> Henry Cavill

List all the people, places, or things leading up to and during your performances that unnerve you, rattle your cage and distract you from the task in hand. You might also like to refer back to the list of things that drain your energy, which you completed in the Self-Management section.

Look at the above list and note down the things where you do have some control over the situation. What strategies can you put in place to eliminate, avoid or minimize their negative effect?

THINGS YOU CAN CONTROL	STRATEGIES TO DEAL WITH THEM

For those things that you cannot control, how can you deal with them resourcefully and positively? What mindset, attitude or approach will help you deal with the people, place or thing so that the negative impact is minimized?

THINGS YOU CAN NOT CONTROL	STRATEGIES TO DEAL WITH THEM

Increase in stress, decrease in performance

How many of you can relate to when you are just about to start a competition or undertake a challenge, and are feeling somewhat nervous and stressed? You may be about to do something you have never done before or wonder whether you have prepared enough. As the nervous mental stress rises, so does the tension in the physical body. The net result is that you are less able to perform physically than if you were relaxed. On a mental level, you think less clearly, logically and analytically than if you were relaxed.

Butler and Hope (1995) have an excellent analogy for getting the balance just right. They describe the pressure of a car tire. If the pressure is correct, you have a smooth ride. However, if the pressure is too low, you feel all the bumps in the road, and if the pressure is too high, you bounce around and easily swing out of control. From a performance perspective, there is an equally fine balance.

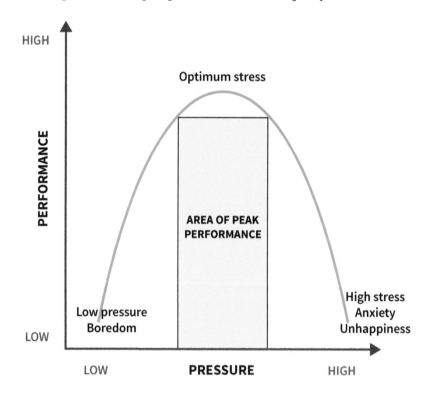

Figure 1: The effects of stress on performance.

It is therefore important to develop an awareness of stress and it's effect on performance (see Figure 1 above), followed on by where tension is held in the body.

To help you recognize what stress and tension feel like, do an internal body check. Notice how you are sitting. How comfortable are you feeling? Are you feeling balanced and square or tilted to one side? How do your shoulders feel? Are they relaxed or somewhat tense?

How is your breathing? Do you feel some tension or do you feel calm and relaxed? Now bring your attention to around your eyes and imagine letting go of any tension there. Did you notice any shift? Make a few notes for yourself as a reminder of what tension feels like in the body, in detail, and how it feels to release that tension.

> *I think it's healthy for a person to be nervous. It means you care – that you work hard and want to give a great performance. You just have to channel that nervous energy into the show.*
>
> Beyonce Knowles

This internal body check is simply to assist you in taking notice of what is going on within. By taking time to do this check at different times and in different situations, it will help you to develop a greater awareness of your physical body and where you might be holding any tension.

Write down any thoughts from this experience and any reminders that will help you in the future.

Progressive muscle relaxation

This technique is to help you progressively, and very consciously, relax all of your muscles. This in turn will help to calm any nerves and assist in improving your performance. We often hold stress and tension in the body in our day-to-day lives without even realizing it because it can become the norm. Then, when we get into a performance situation that stress and tension rises. Let's do a few warm up exercises to get you going.

Start off by doing a quick scan of your body to see whether you are holding any tension. Just like you did in the previous exercise.

Now, to illustrate the effect that tight, tense muscles have, much like when you are holding stress, take a moment to tense all of your muscles. Contract all the muscles in your legs, your arms, your abdomen, your shoulders, and even your face.

Try doing the movements you do in your sport. How easy is it for you to move when you are tight and tense like this?

Relax and release all of this tension, and do the movements again. How different is it for you to move when you are tense and tight as opposed to when you are relaxed?

What thoughts or reminders might you give to yourself to relax and release stress and tension in the body? Where do you hold the most tension? Where do you feel the biggest relief when you release the tension?

Progressive muscle relaxation exercise

This exercise is to heighten your awareness of what stress and tension feel like in the body, and what it feels like when you relax and release.

Start by bringing your attention to your breath and notice your chest and abdomen as you inhale and exhale. Now bring your attention to your feet. Contract the muscles in your feet, hold for five seconds and then release.

Slowly move your attention to your calves. Contract the muscles, hold for five seconds and then release. Continue to progress up the body, focusing on one area at a time: the thighs, the abdomen, the chest, the arms, the neck and shoulders, the face and lastly the eyes.

As you contract and release each muscle group, notice the difference between how you feel when the muscles are contracted and when they are relaxed. With practice, you can do a quick scan of the body to sense where you might be holding any tension, and then release it.

Write any notes or thoughts about this experience. What do you need as a reminder to use this technique?

One conscious breath

This breathing exercise is another relaxation technique that you can use during your performances to help bring about a calm and relaxed state.

When we are under stress and pressure, we generally breathe shallowly; we are breathing in shorter breaths and not exhaling fully. This then triggers the 'fight or flight stress response' and makes stress levels even worse in both the body and the mind. By learning to make your exhalations longer than your inhalations (2:1 ratio is a good ratio

> *Remember that with any meditation technique it should not be pursued with a grim determination to 'get it right'. The point is to cultivate openness, relaxation and awareness.*
>
> Andrew Weil

to try out), the body responds by lowering your heart rate, dropping your blood pressure and relaxing your muscles, and will generally signal to your body that all is well.

To practice this 2:1 breathing, take a breath in through your nose and out through your mouth. When you breathe in, imagine the air filling up your abdomen (before your chest) and expanding it naturally. Breathe in to a count of say five (you need to find what is a comfortable number) and then exhale slowly to a count of 10 (or double your in-breath number).

To make this deep breathing exercise even more effective, imagine that with each exhalation you are releasing all the tension from your body. Get a real sense of how this feels as you experience the muscles actually relaxing. You only have to do this conscious breathing for about one or two minutes to have a noticeable effect on how you feel.

In a performance situation, you may not have one or two minutes to do this type of breathing. However, by regularly practicing the technique, and experiencing the feelings of relaxation and release in the body, you will be able to achieve this state simply by one conscious breath. Much like an anchor or your own internal light switch, where all you have to do is flick the switch for the light to go on, you can take one conscious breath to feel the feelings you have practiced.

Write any notes or thoughts about this experience. What do you need as a reminder to use this technique?

Grounding and calming

Another relaxation technique is grounding and calming. It is almost as if you are gathering your energy to a central point within your body to then use for the purposes of your performance.

To help you develop an awareness of being grounded, try the following:

- Stand up in an upright and balanced manner; stand up with your weight evenly distributed between your feet and with your arms hanging loosely by your side. Just stand there and bring your attention to your breathing in a relaxed manner.

- Imagine both a horizontal and vertical line running through your body. Imagine that you have a horizontal line dividing your body in half; imagine you have a vertical line dividing your body in half. Where the two lines meet is your center point. Generally, these lines intersect in the middle of your body slightly behind and below your navel.

- Shift your center point. Imagine moving the horizontal line higher and then lower than the center point. Notice what sensations you experience when you shift the line.

- Now, with the horizontal line returned to the center point, imagine shifting the vertical line to the left and then to the right. Notice what sensations you experience when you shift the line.

What did you notice when you played around with shifting the horizontal line up and down? What about shifting the vertical line left and right? What would be most beneficial to you when you do your performance? What do you need as a reminder to use this technique?

Finally …

Developing the ability to relax the physical body, particularly before an important event, will have a positive effect on your performance. By expanding your conscious awareness of how your body feels when you release any tension, it will assist you in recalling it easily and instantly when it matters the most, for example, at the start of a big competition or big performance.

- It is important to get clear on the people, places and things that have a negative effect on your stress levels before your performances.

- Think of strategies as to how you will deal with those negative stressors in anticipation.

- Remember that there is an optimum stress level to help you achieve peak performances.

- Any relaxation technique that eases tension in the mind and the body will help you to perform better, including progressive muscle relaxation, one conscious breath or grounding and calming.

- Stress and tension are inevitable before a performance but having effective strategies to help you reduce the negative impact will make a difference.

Notes and reflections

Here is some space to make any notes after having completed this section. How did you find the process? What insights did you gain? What thoughts do you have?

Nothing can stop the man with the right mental attitude from achieving his goal; nothing on earth can help the man with the wrong mental attitude.

Thomas Jefferson

ROUTINES

Take a moment to think about your morning routine of getting up and out the door for the day. For most of us, it does not take much thought or energy. You are simply on autopilot and do what you need to do; it is pretty simple and straightforward.

Now, think of a time when you had to get up earlier than usual, for example, to attend a breakfast meeting or to catch an early morning flight to go away on holiday.

How did you sleep the night before? What was the difference in getting up and out the door compared to your regular day-to-day routine? Were you on autopilot or worried about things? For most of us, disruptions in our routine mean we do not sleep as well and our stress levels are a bit higher.

When our routines are disrupted, we have to think more about what to do, and when, simply because it is new or different from our familiar pattern. This additional thought can cause some of us to feel increased stress. The more familiar you are with your routine, the more you will go on autopilot and simply do what you need to do. This familiarity will help keep the stress levels lower, and in turn, help improve performances.

Therefore, taking a look at what makes up your routine to keep you calm, focused and able to perform is one of the key elements to achieving peak levels of performance.

We are what we repeatedly do.
Excellence, then, is not an act, but a habit.
Aristotle

Past performances

To help you develop your own personal routine, the first step is to reflect and gather information related to past performances. By examining what you have done before, you can start putting together the elements for your next big performance.

Begin this process by recalling some of your past performances – both good and not so good. Write down all the things you undertook to get yourself ready, prepared and to the start of your event. This is like a timeline of all the things you did. You might begin with the day before and the activities you performed and the actions you took. Note down all the preparation, the organization, even what you ate and how much sleep you had.

All these questions are meant as prompts to help you think about what you did for different performances. By drawing up a list of all the things you carried out that contributed to a good performance, you can then use it again when you want to achieve yet another good performance.

This list might include elements such as your food intake on the day before and the day of the competition, the amount of rest you had or the people that were around you.

- What sorts of activities did you do? What was the balance between resting and other activities?

- What foods did you eat or not eat?

- When did you prepare all your clothes and equipment to take to the event? How did you know what to take?

- What people, places or things were you around? How did they influence or impact on your ability to stay focused?

- How did you get to the event and who was responsible for figuring out directions and logistics?

- On the morning of the event, when did you eat before the start? What did you eat?

- What specifically did you do to warm up and prepare for the event? Who was around you?

Your pre-event routine is important and you might need more paper. Make sure you write out all the steps and details that you have done before your events to help you create your perfect pre-event routine for the future.

Examining the past performances

Now that you have listed all the activities and actions leading up to the performances, it is time to examine them.

Look carefully at and reflect upon everything you did that contributed towards your performance. Ask yourself whether they made a positive contribution or had a negative effect. Simply put, did it help or hinder what you did?

After that, you need to come up with some ideas about how you can ensure to repeat the positive things and either change, eliminate or minimize the negative things for the next time.

This examination will start forming elements for your pre-event routine and your own personal 'recipe for success'.

ACTIVITY / ACTION	HELP + / HINDER –	STRATEGY

Developing your routine

Once you have examined the activities and actions that helped or hindered your past performances, it is time to develop your own personal 'recipe for success', which lists out the essential constituents of your routine.

A pre-event checklist is an actual list of everything that you need to do before the day of the event. The overall aim of having a checklist is to ensure that everything you need to do or think about is done. Plus, you do not have to worry about missing or forgetting things.

This checklist might also include your pre-event routine. Much like your morning routine of getting up and going to work, your pre-event routine is hopefully as familiar to you and therefore helps you to stay relaxed. It will tell you what to do on the day of the event in order to assist you to get ready for the start.

For sports-related performances, a pre-event checklist and routine might include the following:

The secret of your future is hidden in your (daily) routine.
Mike Murdoch

Week prior to event

- EATING – Ensure you consume healthy foods that you are used to and that provide quality fuel for your body. Do you want or need to eat specific types of foods leading up to your event? Do you need to bring this yourself or can you get it where you are staying?

- RESTING – Ensure you get sufficient rest, possibly more than normal, before the event. Also, avoid any unnecessary expenditure of energy or activities. Do you need to get additional rest or sleep before your event? How much? How many hours sleep do you like to get to perform at your best?

- EXERCISE – Keep your body moving to maintain flexibility without putting added strain or demands on it. How do you need to adjust your training schedule and taper before the event? Do you need to do some specific stretching or get a massage?

- OTHER ACTIVITIES – Do you need to reduce additional activities that you do, such as walking around visiting a new city before a big event or taking time off work the day before?

- SELF-CARE – Do whatever makes you feel good about yourself and your life. This might mean taking time out for you before a big event or perhaps surrounding yourself with positive, supportive friends. What sorts of activities contribute to your overall sense of well-being? How could you incorporate some of them into your schedule just before the event?

- DISTRACTIONS – Minimize the distractions placed on you. This might mean that you have to isolate yourself away from the normal day-to-day demands of life. What sorts of things do you find distracting and take away from your focus? What could you put in place to minimize these distractions?

- VISUALIZATION EXERCISES – Regularly visualize your perfect event. Include aspects, for example, of the course / landmarks, the arena, the supporters and entertainment, water / feeding stations, when and where to drink and eat. How vividly can you imagine your performances? What will you see, hear and even experience during the event?

- POSITIVE SELF-TALK – Repeat positive self-talk such as 'I have done all the training; I will complete the distance; I feel strong and powerful.' Do you have a written list of positive affirmations that you can review just before you perform? What is on that list?

Day before event

- Arrange all your clothes, food required for pre-, during and post-event. Make sure you have a list of all the things that you might need or want to bring with you, and check them off when you pack.

- Confirm travel arrangements and directions.

- Calculate what time to set the alarm clock to get up and do the necessary things before leaving the house, e.g. time for breakfast, shower, stretching, etc.

- Get breakfast food prepared beforehand as much as possible. For example, all the food and cutlery you need already out on the counter. This will help speed things up in the morning.

- Remind yourself what you are going to do and the sequence of events. This could be similar to a countdown that counts back from when the event starts all the way to when you get up in the morning.

Day of event

- Execute your 'day of event' routine for when you get up and for everything you need to do to get to the event.

- Warm up physically and mentally by doing a stretching routine in a specific sequence and doing your mental rehearsal.

- Plan for loo stops / comfort breaks to use the washroom facilities.

- Review game plan for event – this is your personal strategy for the event and your goals.

- Review lists of positive affirmations and positive statements you can use to turn around any negative dialogue.

During event

- Maintain focus on you, on what you are doing and on your own game plan.

- Do regular assessments to check progress and make adjustments as required. For example, a runner might check how they are feeling in order to decide whether they can change their pace.

- Maintain the positive self-talk to reassure yourself that you have completed all the necessary training to achieve the goal, and that you are strong and healthy.

- Focus on your performance, your effort and your own game plan, rather than the outcome.

Your recipe for success, pre-event routine

Here is where you write out all the things you need to do in the week before the event, the day before the event, the morning of the event, and the actual event to help you be the best you can be. Using the above list as a prompt, develop your own recipe for success of all the things you need to do before your event to get the best performance possible. Make sure to include a list of all the clothes and food that you might need before, during and after the event. Even if your performance goal is outside the sporting arena, many of the above prompts might still apply.

Week before the event

> *There are no secrets to success. It is the result of preparation, hard work, and learning from failure.*
> Colin Powell

Day before the event

Morning of the event

Actual event

You might even start using this checklist and pre-event routine for your training sessions to try them out and see how well they worked for you.

When you have your checklist and implement your pre-event routine, how do you feel at the start of your event? How are your energy levels just prior to and during the event? How much calmer, more focused and ready for action do you feel knowing that you have done all the preparation you need to do?

Finally ...

Routines that are familiar to us are comfortable and there is little stress about them. Therefore, developing your own personal pre-event routine will help you to calm any nerves, leaving you with more energy to pour into your performance. Taking time to examine your past performances, and what worked well and what didn't, will help you to come up with an ideal routine to assist you in being at your best.

- Review your past events and identify all the factors that contributed to your performances.

- Make sure to keep and repeat all those things that had a positive effect and eliminate or adjust those things that had a negative effect on your performance.

- Writing out a checklist of everything you need to do to get organized and prepared will help to reduce worry and stress, and thereby improve performances.

- Everyone's pre-event routine will be unique to them and it is important to find out what works best for you.

- Review the checklist and pre-event routine after each event to analyze whether you need to make any adjustments for the next time.

Notes and reflections

Here is some space to make any notes after having completed this section. How did you find the process? What insights did you gain? What thoughts do you have?

> *Don't wait until everything is just right. It will never be perfect. There will always be challenges, obstacles, and less than perfect conditions. So what? Get started now. With each step you take, you will grow stronger, more skilled, self-confident, and successful.*
> Mark Victor Hansen

FOCUS

Can you recall a time when you were so enthralled with something like a movie, a great conversation or a good book that time just seemed to fly by and you didn't notice it passing? Have you ever worked on a really interesting project and before you realized it, the day was gone?

These types of situations where you are not consciously aware of time passing demonstrate an intense focus on something or someone. Yet, the reality is that more often than not our focus and attention jumps from one thing to the next. Ideally in a performance situation, you want your attention and focus to be entirely on what helps you.

Gallwey (1981) identifies the steps for developing concentration and focus as discipline, interest, absorption and oneness. The discipline to pay attention only to the here and now, and to what is currently present in your environment, is the first step. Next, interest relates to simply being interested in what you are paying attention to, otherwise why pay attention to it in the first instance. The third step is being absorbed in what you are doing, almost to the exclusion of all else that is going on around you; you are fully concentrating on what you are doing; there is no room for any anxiety or fear to enter. This leads onto a sense of 'oneness' and being fully present in the 'now'; nothing else is happening except what you are doing.

Those four simple steps take some practice to develop, but they will have a positive effect on your ability to be absorbed and fully focused when you perform. A good example is children focused on a game where they are so absorbed that they are unaware of the world around them. As athletes, your performance can benefit from developing this same ability.

How often have you started on one task and then picked up something else before coming back to what you first started? Have you ever tried completing several jobs at once, either at work or at home? Did you have a sense that you were not progressing things? Have you ever been chatting with someone on the phone while checking emails or social media? What was that like for you? How did you feel overall with this focusing on several things at once?

Under the pretense of 'multi-tasking', many people actually take longer to complete tasks than had they been able to focus on one thing at a time and complete it.

By the same token, have you ever felt totally absorbed in a task? Did time just seem to fly by? Were you able to exclude any distractions while you got the job done? What was that like for you?

In a performance situation, the ability to focus on one thing at a time and only on task-relevant details will make a big difference to the outcomes you achieve because all your energy, attention and efforts are directed towards a particular outcome.

Developing the ability to maintain your focus is a habit, much like many of the other mental skills in this *Winning Strategies* process. With practice and vigilant attention, you can develop your awareness of where your thoughts are and recognize whether they help or hinder your ability to perform at your best. As soon as you notice that the thoughts are unhelpful, you can shift your attention to those that are more constructive.

One reason so few of us achieve what we truly want is that we never direct our focus; we never concentrate our power. Most people dabble their way through life, never deciding to master anything in particular.

Tony Robbins

Why focus on your focus?

We often do not take the time to think about what we think about, nor do we take time to pay attention to where our focus is. However, in performance situations noticing our thoughts and noticing where our attention is, and deciding whether they are helping or hindering us, can be crucial to ensure a good outcome.

The first step is to identify what is relevant and important to pay attention to. These 'task-relevant' details are your thoughts and where you place your attention as well as your actions and what you do. Naturally, these thoughts and actions need to assist you with your performance rather than detract from it.

Write out a list of the thoughts that you generally have leading up to and during your performance. Also include the actions you take and the people you come into contact with. Then, take a look and evaluate them to determine whether they help or hinder your performance abilities. Do they give you a boost and are focused solely on you, or do they drag you away from your own efforts? If they help, then they are likely to be considered task-relevant.

THOUGHTS	HELP OR HINDER YOUR PERFORMANCE

Developing the habit

The next step is to develop the habit of keeping your focus and attention solely on those task-relevant things and coming up with strategies to deal with any distractions. Inevitably, there will be distractions that take your attention away from what you are doing – be that other competitors in the event, something at home that you need to do or a challenging situation you are currently experiencing elsewhere in your life.

Once you notice your attention has strayed to thoughts that are not related to your performance, you need to bring it back to the task in hand. For example, for an athlete, how you are feeling in your body is a task-relevant detail to be aware of, whereas worrying about the other competitors and how they are doing does not improve your performance and is not task-relevant.

Like many other habits, it is a question of becoming aware and noticing when it is happening, and then gently bringing yourself back on track. With practice, the habit of maintaining focus on what is important will become second nature and the ability to refocus after a distraction will become easier to do.

Whether it is unhelpful thoughts or outside distractions, learning to let them go or turn them around to something more helpful and supportive is critical to effective performances. To help you turn things around when you become distracted, write down what you can focus on instead that will be more positive and constructive.

> *Life is 10% what happens to me and 90% of how I react to it.*
>
> Charles Swindoll

UNHELPFUL THOUGHTS	TURNAROUND MORE HELPFUL THOUGHTS

How stress affects concentration

In addition to exploring whether your thoughts help or hinder your ability to perform, it is also a good thing to understand how stress affects your concentration.

You can start to develop this awareness simply by stopping what you are doing and observing as to what and where you are paying attention. Is your focus on the big picture (broad) or the detail (narrow)? Is your focus on things external (other people and things) or internal (yourself) to you? By developing this awareness in everyday situations, you can then more easily use this skill during your training sessions, and more importantly, in your events.

By noticing where your attention is, you can then begin to see situations where you might need a different kind of attention and shift your focus to an appropriate concentration zone as the situation demands.

When we become stressed, we tend to go back to the zone we are most comfortable in and this might not be appropriate for what you need to do. Notice what happens when you start feeling stressed about something. Where does your attention go? Is it internal or external? Is it broad or narrow?

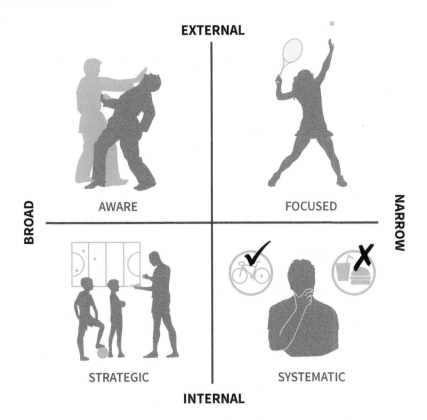

Figure 2: Illustrates the different concentration styles from broad to narrow and external to internal.

For some individuals, their focus and attention retreats to narrow/internal and they focus on their own thoughts and fears. They become so wrapped up in their own thoughts that they are no longer focused on what they should be concentrating on. This is often where mistakes are made. Yet, if they were able to bring their attention to outside of themselves, they might not become so worried or stressed and perform better.

In addition to stress affecting your concentration, it also affects your performance. Nideffer (1976) illustrates the effects of stress on performances, see Figure 3 below.

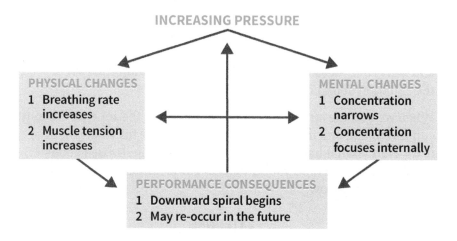

Figure 3: Effects of pressure on performance.

Recognizing how you react in high stress situations will help you to take steps to ensure that you change your attention and focus to what is more appropriate for what you are about to do.

Dealing with distractions

It is inevitable that you will encounter distractions prior to and during your events. Therefore, learning how to deal with potential distractions will help you to maintain your tunnel-like vision and to focus on what is necessary.

Distractions might be people, places or things. They might also be your own thoughts. Paying attention to these distractions will most likely increase your stress levels and might not help you perform to your best. It is therefore important to focus on those things that you can control and let go of those things that you have no control over.

By becoming clear on the things that assist your performance, those task-relevant details, you can help yourself to stay focused on them. However, your mind may at times wander off to non-task-relevant things because that is human nature.

> *To conquer frustration, one must remain intensely focused on the outcome, not the obstacles.*
>
> T.F. Hodge

One way to practice focusing on task-related details is during your training sessions. Challenge yourself to pay attention to one thing during your practice. It could be anything that positively contributes to your performance. In the case of a runner, they could focus on their breathing or their posture. In the case of a golfer, they could focus on how stable their hips are during the swing. The focus area will be different for each athlete and each person depending on what they perform.

Decide what you want to focus on and each time you notice that you are not paying attention to this element, bring yourself back on track and refocus on what you have chosen to pay attention to. With practice, the noticing and refocusing will become easier.

Write out a list of the common distractions you encounter at your events and think of some ideas as to how you can manage, eliminate or avoid them.

> *Concentration is the secret of strength.*
> Ralph Waldo Emerson

DISTRACTIONS	HOW TO MANAGE, ELIMINATE OR AVOID

Letting go of mistakes

Dwelling on mistakes is a focus issue. When some performers make a mistake, they brood over it and beat themselves up internally or somehow act out externally. They may have put the ball wide during a penalty shot, committed a foul or missed a putt and then they seem to lose it. They are unable to regain their composure and often spiral downwards even further making more mistakes and performing badly as a result. Effectively, they have held onto that mistake and not let it go.

During a performance, it is important to let go of any previous mistakes or mishaps and move on. Dwelling on the past and the fact that you may have missed a shot, fumbled a ball or were offside, does not do you or the team you may be playing for any good.

Are there any particular kinds of mistakes that you find hard to let go? How does holding onto them help you? What do you need to do to remind yourself to let go of mistakes? What can you say to yourself to be able to let them go? What needs to happen for you to return your attention to being fully present in the moment and to what you are doing?

Practice your focus

For those of you who practice meditation, you may know how challenging it can be to refocus the mind after it has wandered. Even though we intend to focus on one thing, we can suddenly find random thoughts popping up such as what we have to do later that day, what we are going to eat or even the discussion we have just had with someone. This can happen despite repeated practice. However, the skill is to acknowledge these thoughts when they do appear and then bring our attention back to what we were initially focused on.

To start this practice and develop the skill of focusing, you can try a simple exercise. Focus on 10 breaths, placing 100% of your attention on your in-breath and your out-breath to the count of 10. How easy or challenging was that? For many of you, random thoughts might have popped up even though you were trying to focus on just 10 breaths. This demonstrates how challenging it can be to focus on one thing alone.

Similarly, when you try to focus on your performance, random thoughts will most likely pop up. If you find it challenging to focus on taking 10 breaths, you can imagine what it will be like when you try to focus for the duration of a match, a competition or any other performance.

Like any skill, you can improve your ability to focus on task-relevant details with practice.

Start this practice of maintaining focus on one thing, such as your breath, for the duration of one minute and then gradually increase its length by a minute at a time. Observe the effect it has on what you do when you start and when you increase your time. Note down what the experience is like.

What helps you to bring your focus back to the task in hand? What can you do to practice this skill of focus?

Finally …

Paying attention to what you focus on during a performance is another critical element in your mental skills toolkit. You may have many random thoughts running through your head, but by observing where you are placing your attention you can become more aware and mindful of the thoughts that are helpful and those that are not.

- By noticing what sorts of things you are thinking about before and during your performances, and which ones are helpful to you, you can more easily bring your attention back to only those thoughts that will assist you.

- A simply question to ask is 'help or hinder?' Do those thoughts help you or do they hinder you? Only pay attention those that help.

- Errors and mistakes are usually inevitable; the key is to simply let them go rather than dwell on them.

- Stress can affect your ability to focus on task-relevant details or to see critical performance indicators, so recognize what happens to your attention when you become stressed and have strategies in place to re-focus.

- Practice the skill of focus through a daily practice of something like meditation. This will help you deal with those random thoughts that jump in and enable you to bring your attention back to the task in hand.

Notes and reflections

Here is some space to make any notes after having completed this section. How did you find the process? What insights did you gain? What thoughts do you have?

Don't give in to your fears. If you do, you won't be able to talk to your heart.
Paulo Coelho

Additional notes

Section 4
Post-Event Review

The previous steps in the *Winning Strategies* process all contribute towards raising your performances to greater heights. If you are going to put yourself in similar situations in the future, it is best to complete this last step. A Post-Event Review completes the peak performance cycle and helps you to do even better the next time you have a comparable event and when you want to improve your results. It might also give you some thoughts and ideas about other performance situations where you want to be at your best.

The first step in your review is to re-assess the original goals you set for yourself. This is followed by an evaluation of your mental preparation, and all the skills and techniques you developed for performing at your events. By completing an objective review, you can identify what worked well and what didn't work so well.

Ideally, at your next performance, you will be able to repeat the things that were effective and avoid those that were not. Each time you go through this performance review process, you can refine, re-adjust and realign what you need to do to improve or even completely change or eliminate things.

Whether the performance is in the sporting arena or elsewhere in your life, you can use this review process to examine things in greater depth.

After you finish your performance event, you may either be on a high or a low depending on the outcome that you achieved. It is therefore not recommended to do a post-event review immediately. Allow yourself some time to let your emotions return to a more balanced state in order to gain a better perspective. Talking things through with a coach, trusted friend or mental preparation coach can also help with being more objective.

Overall, doing this review will help you to raise your game and your performances to greater heights each time you go out.

REVIEW, REFLECT AND PLAN

> *You can't make up for lost time. You can only do better in the future.*
> Ashley Ormon

Once you have finished your big event, it is important that you take time to enjoy the achievement. Take pride in all the hard work and effort it took to get you there. Savor the sense of accomplishment in having picked a goal, made a plan and worked that plan.

There will be many factors that contribute to the results you achieve. Sometimes the results will be what you expect and at other times, they won't. By taking some time to review what did and didn't work well, you can identify the elements that contributed to your outcome. Effectively, you are creating your own 'recipe for success' whereby you have all the ingredients to help you produce great performances.

As this Post-Event Review section is an appraisal of all the previous steps in the *Winning Strategies* process, it will only contain the questions rather than any descriptions or details. Please refer to the relevant sections if you want further clarification.

Continue, stop or do

What are you doing now that **you can continue** doing in order to perform at your best?

What are you doing now that **you have to stop** doing in order to perform at your best?

What are you not doing now that **you could be doing** in order to perform at your best?

GETTING STARTED ...
FOR THE NEXT TIME

This initial section is about building strong foundations in your life so that you can go on to perform at your best. It looks at your goals and motivation, your values and beliefs, your time and energy management, and finally, where your goals fit in with everything else in your life.

Goals and outcomes

Did you establish clearly defined, and written out, SMART goals? Were they Specific, Measurable, Achievable, Realistic and Timely? Were they stated positively? How could they be different the next time?

> *Nothing is impossible, the word itself says, 'I'm possible!'*
> Audrey Hepburn

Did you have several goals in relation to the overall big goal? Having more goals will give you more opportunities to 'tick the boxes' for success. What other goals could you have identified to focus on and ensure greater success?

Did you set performance goals, rather than outcome goals? Whereas you have personal control over performance goals, you do not for outcome goals, such as a specific time or placing. What performance goals can you set for the next time?

Values and beliefs

What are the reasons you are doing what you are doing?

What benefits will achieving the outcome give you?

What do you need to believe in order to do what you want to do?

> *Believe you can and you're halfway there.*
> Theodore Roosevelt

Where might you have some limiting beliefs and how can you dispel them?

Self-management

What people, places and things drain your energy? Which ones make you feel uplifted or recharged? Were there any unexpected people, places or things that impacted on your energy levels? What were they?

What mechanisms can you put in place to minimize the negative effects of what drains you?

How can you ensure you have sufficient contact with those things that help you feel recharged?

How effective were your personal boundaries in managing your time, energy and attention? What could you do differently?

Life balance

> *What I've learned is that life is a balance between idealism and realism.*
>
> Peter Hook

Looking at all the important areas in your life, how does your goal fit in with these, and also your other roles and responsibilities?

Are there any adjustments that need to be made to your priorities or to the time you spend on different activities?

Do you need to create clearer boundaries between different areas of your life in order to do your preparation and training? How have you clearly communicated these boundaries to others?

Can you enlist the help and support of someone, which will enable you to do what you need to do more easily? Who are they and how might you approach them?

MENTAL PREPARATION ... FLEXING YOUR MUSCLES

This section is about building and working on the mental skills in advance of your performance, which will benefit you and enable you to go on to perform at your best on the day. These skills can equally be used elsewhere in your life.

Confidence

> *You gain strength, courage and confidence by every experience in which you really stop to look fear in the face. You must do the thing you think you cannot do.*
>
> Eleanor Roosevelt

How confident were you feeling before other events that went well? Describe these situations and how you were feeling.

What sorts of people, places or things had a negative influence on your confidence? What were they saying or doing to contribute towards that feeling?

What sorts of people, places or things had a positive influence on your confidence? What were they saying or doing to contribute towards that feeling?

What does the feeling of confidence look and feel like to you? Imagine what it is like. Imagine your posture, how you are standing, how you are moving and what sorts of things you are saying to yourself.

From your confidence 'resume', which are the events and situations that really stand out for you? Which ones give you a positive, uplifting confidence boost?

Internal dialogue

What sorts of things do you say to yourself? It is helpful to actually write these down so you can see, rather than simply hear, what is being said.

> *Every waking moment we talk to ourselves about the things we experience and, in turn, control the way we feel and act.*
>
> John Limbo

How can you turn any negative commentary into something more positive and supportive? What sorts of things could you say instead?

Were there particular situations where there was more internal chatter? Less internal chatter? Recognizing the typical situations that trigger negative internal chatter can help you to prepare strategies to deal with them in the future.

Mental rehearsal

How often did you visualize your performance before your event and what sorts of aspects were contained within it? How can you increase the intensity of the experience from your visualization? What colors can be more vivid? What sensations in the body more intense? What words will you hear yourself and others say?

How vivid was your visualization? What adjustments could you make to increase the rich experience, including what you would feel like, see and hear?

What types of scenarios can you include when handling difficult situations such as when things are not going to plan or as expected? Imagine the experiences and imagine yourself handling them easily and effortlessly.

EVENT PERFORMANCE ... SWITCHING IT ON

This section helps you develop the skills that you will be drawing upon during your actual performance. Much like the skills in the previous section, you can use them elsewhere in your life.

Relaxation

What can you do to remain calm and relaxed prior to and during your event? How does this feel in each major part of your body?

> *Practice isn't the thing you do once you're good. It's the thing you do that makes you good.*
> Malcolm Gladwell

When you notice an increase in tension, what can you do to relax?

Do any people, places or things increase, or decrease, your sense of stress and tension? What can you do to help yourself remain calm and relaxed?

Where can you practice more of the relaxation exercises? Make sure you practice them outside the pressured event arena so you know they work and can call upon them when necessary.

Routines

What did you include in your pre-event checklist and routine? Are there any changes that could be made?

How effective was using your pre-event checklist to how you felt and how you performed? What might make it even more effective?

In what ways did your routine help you get physically and mentally prepared for your event? How did you feel going into the event? What might you do differently the next time?

Focus

> *Don't dwell on what went wrong. Instead, focus on what to do next. Spend your energies on moving forward toward finding the answer.*
>
> Denis Waitley

What are the task-relevant things to place your attention on? Where was your focus just before and during the event? Were there any non-task-relevant things you paid attention to and what were they? How did this contribute towards your performance? Did it help or hinder?

What type of focus is most needed in your performance? Broad or narrow? Internal or external? What would help to remind you of where you need to place your attention?

What strategies do you have in place to minimize or deal with distractions?

Who can you ask to help and support you in maintaining your focus – be that for training or during competitions?

SUMMARY

Here are some more questions just to help round off your review.

> *Be thankful for what you have; you'll end up having more. If you concentrate on what you don't have, you will never, ever have enough.*
>
> Oprah Winfrey

What can you do to make your next performance even better?

What are the strategies that work for you that you could repeat? What are the tactics that did not work and could be adjusted or replaced?

How did you rate your performance (1 to 10, ten being the best)?

What actions contribute towards supporting you to be the very best at all times?

After your performance, what new goals can you set?

> *Maybe the journey isn't so much about becoming anything. Maybe it's about un-becoming everything that isn't really you, so you can be who you were meant to be in the first place.*
>
> Unknown

Winning Strategies Summary – Checklist

Here is a quick at-a-glance checklist as a reminder of the *Winning Strategies* process.

GETTING STARTED		
Goals and motivation	What do you want to achieve and what benefit will you gain?	
Values and beliefs	What is important about achieving this goal and what difference will it make in your life? What do you need to believe to achieve it?	
Self-management	How can you maximize the positive effects of people, places and things that help you perform? How can you minimize any negatives?	
Life balance	How does your goal fit in with the other important areas in your life? Does anything need to shift?	

MENTAL PREPARATION		
Confidence	What does confidence look and feel like to you, and how could you tap into it for your performance?	
Internal dialogue	How can you turn up the volume on the positive things you say? How can you mute or dispel any negative things?	
Mental rehearsal	How real can your movie be of you performing at your best? What do you see, hear and feel?	

EVENT PERFORMANCE		
Relaxation	How can you maintain a sense of relaxation? What do you need to remember to take one conscious breath?	
Routines	What is contained in your pre-event checklist and routine? What things can you keep, alter or discard for the next time?	
Focus	What are the task-relevant elements that help you perform? How can you bring your attention back to them?	

POST-EVENT REVIEW		
Review, reflect and plan	What can be repeated the next time and what could be modified?	

CONCLUSION

The journey towards raising your performances is an exciting and challenging one. Of course, you can do the technical preparation and have the physical capabilities, and achieve great outcomes. However, by considering the mental preparation aspects in addition, you can achieve outstanding results. Like the physical aspects of training, it takes practice and effort, as well as consistent vigilance to monitor your thoughts and train them towards helping you be the best you can be.

It is important to recognize that your peak performance levels may be very different from another person's levels. We are all individual and unique. For one person, their goal may be monumental, whereas for another, it might be like a warm-up. As an example, take someone just recovering from a serious injury. For them, merely being able to walk unaided or to run around the track without any discomfort may be a major milestone. From the initial step of getting started and deciding to 'go for it', you can benefit from clarifying your goals and your motivation, and your values and beliefs, as well as identifying how a particular goal fits in with the other important areas in your life. Ensuring that you maintain a healthy balance in all your activities and responsibilities contributes towards you having the time and energy to develop your preparation. These initial steps are the foundations for your journey towards achieving peak performance levels.

All the mental preparation you do beforehand will influence the outcome on the day of your big performance event. So, focusing on the mind element will help. Being mentally prepared for your event means that you develop increased confidence in what you are going to do. You can turn down the volume or mute any negative self-talk and turn up the volume on the positive, supportive comments. You can also mentally rehearse your entire event from start to finish, as if you are directing your own movie where you are the producer. This tricks the brain into thinking that it has already done the performance – 'been there, done that'!

Then, on the big day, you need to be switched on. Developing the ability to relax and to use one conscious breath will help calm those nerves, clear your head of any distracting thoughts and aid you in performing even better. Establishing routines helps because you can go on autopilot and do not have to think too much about what you are doing; you simply do it. Also, by knowing what to focus on and knowing what task-relevant things assist you to perform, you can let go of mistakes and focus on purely doing what you need to do.

Once you have completed your event, it is important to take time to recognize your achievements and take what learning you can from the experience. By reviewing and reflecting on what you accomplished and identifying the elements that contributed to the results, you can then develop your own template or 'recipe for success' for the next time.

Now, consider where else you would like to achieve peak levels of performance. You can take all that you have learned throughout this *Winning Strategies* process and apply it to other areas in your life where you want to be the best you can be. Whether it is when you are working on a significant project or about to make a big presentation at work, going for an interview, conducting an important meeting or having a major discussion with someone, you can use all the steps in this process to help you.

Using these *Winning Strategies* steps will assist you in creating a mindset for success and help align your thoughts, your actions, and your energy towards realizing your greatest potential. With every training session, and every day, consider what you are doing and how you are doing it. Then, ask yourself do my actions help or hinder me towards achieving my goal?

It takes practice and vigilance, yet with attention and regular effort, you can do it. You can develop your mental toughness skills and be like a gold medal winner.

> *Success is achieved by ordinary people with extraordinary determination.*
> Zig Ziglar

ABOUT MIDGIE

Midgie Thompson specializes in 'Inspiring Excellence' in individuals and teams. She helps them develop performance skills by combining mental toughness techniques with balanced lifestyle choices.

Midgie founded Bright Futures Coaching Ltd in 2003 and has been providing motivational, mental performance and personal development coaching ever since. The company also offers business performance, management and communication skills courses.

Midgie regularly writes for sporting and business journals, and is a media spokesperson on mental preparation skills, peak performance, goal setting, motivation and confidence building. She also teaches at the University of Brighton and provides community engagement support and coaching advice for the Mind Tools Career Excellence Club.

She has coached athletes at all levels from amateur to world championship, and worked with people in the business world up to managing director level. For her one-to-one coaching sessions, Midgie takes advantage of technology and coaches individuals via Skype all over the world.

Midgie currently lives in Nice, France, and is a year-round open water swimmer and recreational triathlete.

> *Gratitude unlocks the fullness of life. It turns what we have into enough, and more. It turns denial into acceptance, chaos to order, confusion to clarity. It can turn a meal into a feast, a house into a home, a stranger into a friend. Gratitude makes sense of our past, brings peace for today and creates a vision for tomorrow.*
> Melody Beattie